The BOARD BUILDING *Cycle*

Nine Steps to Finding, Recruiting, and Engaging Nonprofit Board Members

Second Edition

by Berit M. Lakey

BOARDSOURCE®
Building Effective Nonprofit Boards

Library of Congress Cataloging-in-Publication Data

Lakey, Berit M.

The board building cycle : nine steps to finding, recruiting, and engaging nonprofit board members / by Berit M. Lakey. — 2nd ed.

    p. cm.

Previous ed. had Sandra R. Hughes as the first author.

ISBN 1-58686-093-3 pbk.

1. Boards of directors--United States. 2. Nonprofit organizations—United States. I. Title.

HD2745.H84 2007
658.4'22--dc22

2007012517

Published by BoardSource
1828 L Street, NW, Suite 900
Washington, DC 20036

BOARDSOURCE®
Building Effective Nonprofit Boards

BoardSource, formerly the National Center for Nonprofit Boards, is the premier resource for practical information, tools and best practices, training, and leadership development for board members of nonprofit organizations worldwide. Through our highly acclaimed programs and services, BoardSource enables organizations to fulfill their missions by helping build strong and effective nonprofit boards.

BoardSource provides assistance and resources to nonprofit leaders through workshops, training, and our extensive Web site, www.boardsource.org. A team of BoardSource governance consultants works directly with nonprofit leaders to design specialized solutions to meet organizations' needs and assists nongovernmental organizations around the world through partnerships and capacity building. As the world's largest, most comprehensive publisher of materials on nonprofit governance, BoardSource offers a wide selection of books, videotapes, CDs, and online tools. BoardSource also hosts the BoardSource Leadership Forum, bringing together governance experts, board members, and chief executives of nonprofit organizations from around the world.

Created out of the nonprofit sector's critical need for governance guidance and expertise, BoardSource is a 501c3 nonprofit organization that has provided practical solutions to nonprofit organizations of all sizes in diverse communities. In 2001, BoardSource changed its name from the National Center for Nonprofit Boards to better reflect its mission. Today, BoardSource has approximately 11,000 members and has served more than 75,000 nonprofit leaders.

For more information, please visit our Web site, www.boardsource.org, e-mail us at mail@boardsource.org, or call us at 800-883-6262.

Have You Used These BoardSource Resources?

VIDEOS

Meeting the Challenge: An Orientation to Nonprofit Board Service
Speaking of Money: A Guide to Fundraising for Nonprofit Board Members

BOOKS

The Board Chair Handbook
Managing Conflicts of Interest: A Primer for Nonprofit Boards
Driving Strategic Planning: A Nonprofit Executive's Guide
Taming the Troublesome Board Member
The Nonprofit Dashboard: A Tool for Tracking Progress
Presenting: Nonprofit Financials
Meet Smarter: A Guide to Better Nonprofit Board Meetings
The Nonprofit Policy Sampler, Second Edition
Getting the Best from Your Board: An Executive's Guide to a Successful Partnership
Nonprofit Board Answer Book: Practical Guide for Board Members and Chief Executives
The Source: Twelve Principles of Governance That Power Exceptional Boards
The Nonprofit Legal Landscape
Self-Assessment for Nonprofit Governing Boards
Assessment of the Chief Executive
Fearless Fundraising
The Nonprofit Board's Guide to Bylaws
Understanding Nonprofit Financial Statements
Transforming Board Structure: Strategies for Committees and Task Forces

THE GOVERNANCE SERIES

1. *Ten Basic Responsibilities of Nonprofit Boards*
2. *Financial Responsibilities of Nonprofit Boards*
3. *Structures and Practices of Nonprofit Boards*
4. *Fundraising Responsibilities of Nonprofit Boards*
5. *Legal Responsibilities of Nonprofit Boards*
6. *The Nonprofit Board's Role in Setting and Advancing the Mission*
7. *The Nonprofit Board's Role in Planning and Evaluation*
8. *How To Help Your Board Govern More and Manage Less*
9. *Leadership Roles in Nonprofit Governance*

For an up-to-date list of publications and information about current prices, membership, and other services, please call BoardSource at 800-883-6262 or visit our Web site at www.boardsource.org.

Contents

Preface

The concepts presented in this book have been developed through my many years of experience as a board consultant, board member, and chief executive of nonprofit organizations as well as by other experts in the field, including other BoardSource consultants. These ideas have been field tested with scores of organizations from differing mission areas, both large and small. Examples of how different organizations have responded to the challenges involved in building strong boards are provided throughout the book. Some come from specific organizations while others are composites based on what has been learned from a variety of boards.

This book was first published in 2000 and was co-authored by Sandra R. Hughes, Berit M. Lakey, and Marla J. Bobowick. It built on the work of Judith Grummon Nelson, who in 1993 wrote *Six Keys to Recruiting, Orienting, and Involving Nonprofit Board Members* (BoardSource). Since then, thousands of boards have used the tools in these publications to help guide them through the board building process. I am grateful for the foundation built in 1993, but also for all that I have learned from Sandra and Marla who continue to share their experience and wisdom with me and with boards around the country. Like me, they are heartened by finding that boards of nonprofit organizations are now increasingly seeking to discover how to become more strategic assets to their organizations. I would also like to acknowledge the contributions of Outi Flynn, who has proved to be a valuable resource for me during my work on this edition of the book and whenever I needed information about some obscure governance issue. And to my editors, Claire Perella, who gently kicked me into action and Janis Johnston, who graciously and knowledgeably took over when Claire moved on to new challenges elsewhere: Thanks for your ability to simplify and clarify!

Introduction

As we have seen, the matter of selection goes deeper than the choice of the 'right' people. There are indeed some men and women who, because of innate capacity or wealth or position in the community, would be welcome additions to almost any board. Most of the time, however, the selection of board members should be made by deciding who is 'right' for a particular board, who can strengthen it, and who can give it the distinctive qualities that it needs at the present moment.

— Cyril O. Houle

It is a scenario repeated all too often. Annual elections are coming up, the board hastily forms a nominating committee, and members scramble to find willing candidates to fill the open positions, often choosing less-than-ideal replacements in the interest of time.

The trouble is, potential good board members are in short supply. Every year thousands of board positions need to be filled throughout this country. Every year more and more people decide that the myriad of demands on their time makes it impossible to accept the invitation for board service. Every year organizations in every community compete for good board members. Every year many will settle for finding enough people willing to serve whether or not they are the right people for the job.

But the job of building the board is more than just filling slots. It is about being strategic in the way a board looks at its composition and its operations. Rapid changes in the nonprofit sector have required that organizations take a closer look at not only how the business of the organization is conducted, but how decisions are made and by whom. Scandals in both the for-profit and the nonprofit sectors have led to increased attention by public media as well as by state and federal authorities.

An effective board is becoming a strategic necessity, not only a legal requirement. The most effective boards — those whose members are deeply committed to the organization's mission, who bring expertise in key areas, and who represent diverse points of view — evolve over time through careful planning. Should a pivotal board member suddenly depart, the board is not caught off-guard because it continually works to identify and cultivate potential candidates.

THE WORK OF THE GOVERNANCE COMMITTEE

Traditionally, the committee that fills the role of recruiting new board members has been called a "nominating committee." In this book I will use the term "governance committee" instead, thus broadening the group's scope and expanding its importance. This committee tackles one of the principal responsibilities of the board: to ensure that the board continuously strives to be as effective as it can be.

The governance committee is more proactive than the traditional nominating committee. That may mean recommending, due to a strategic shift in the organization, that a new board member with special expertise be brought on to the board. It could also mean asking another person to step down to make way for someone with skill sets more appropriate to the growing, changing organization. It may mean taking notice of board malaise waning attendance or declining discussions and recommending corrective action. Such action could include calling for an executive session or conducting a board self-assessment to discover the root of the problem and to determine what to do to turn things around. The governance committee's work is vital to the health of the board and of the organization. It is the board's mechanism for looking after itself. In their book *Improving the Performance of Governing Boards*, Richard P. Chait, Thomas P. Holland, and Barbara E. Taylor

BOARD ROLES AND RESPONSIBILITIES

Establish Direction

- Develop and maintain focus on mission and vision.

- Establish strategic direction.

- Delegate authority for organizational management.

- Articulate, safeguard, model, and promote organizational values.

Ensure Resources

- Develop policies related to the generation of financial resources.

- Ensure that the necessary resources are made available for implementation of the mission.

- Ensure that the organization has the leadership needed at both the staff level and the board level.

Provide Oversight

- Establish financial policies and ensure accountability.

- Ensure compliance with applicable laws and ethical standards.

- Monitor progress toward strategic goals and evaluate outcomes

INDIVIDUAL BOARD MEMBER RESPONSIBILITIES

- Attend all board and committee meetings and functions, such as special events.

- Stay informed about the organization's mission, services, policies, and programs.

- Review agenda and supporting materials prior to board and committee meetings.

- Serve on committees and offer to take on special assignments.

emphasize the central role of this committee — which they call the trusteeship committee: "For many boards, the trusteeship committee or board affairs committee, plays the most pivotal role in board development. With a broader charge than the typical nominating committee, the trusteeship committee bears explicit responsibility for board development, education, and assessment, as well as the recruitment of new members."

The Board Building Cycle emphasizes the key role of the governance committee and presents an overview and a road map to this process, discussing each phase in detail. The book can be used to prompt board members to rethink their entire board development process. Or it can be the basis for a mini self-assessment by asking

- Make a personal financial contribution to the organization.

- Inform others about the organization.

- Suggest possible nominees to the board who can make significant contributions to the work of the board and the organization.

- Keep up-to-date on developments in the organization's field.

- Follow conflict-of-interest and confidentiality policies.

- Refrain from making special requests of the staff.

- Assist the board in carrying out its fiduciary responsibilities, such as reviewing annual financial statements.

PERSONAL CHARACTERISTICS NEEDED IN BOARD MEMBERS

- Ability to listen, analyze, think clearly and creatively, and work well with individuals and groups.

- Willingness to prepare for and participate in board and committee meetings, ask relevant questions, take responsibility and follow through on a given assignment, contribute personal and financial resources in a generous way according to circumstances, open doors in the community, and evaluate oneself.

- Willingness to develop certain skills, such as cultivating and soliciting funds, cultivating and recruiting board members and other volunteers, reading and understanding financial statements, learning more about the substantive program areas of the organization.

- Possess honesty; sensitivity; tolerance of differing views; a friendly, responsive, and patient approach; community-building skills; personal integrity; a sense of values; concern for your nonprofit's development; and a sense of humor.

Adapted from *Six Keys to Recruiting, Orienting, and Involving Nonprofit Board Members* by Judith Grummon Nelson, BoardSource, 1993.

members to identify parts of this cycle that are noticeably strong or weak, then discussing plans for making improvements.

This book is intended not only for charitable organizations where the board is charged with selecting its own members, but also for organizations where the authority to appoint new board members rests elsewhere. In those cases, such as associations whose members elect the board, the governance committee can use this book to assess the organization's needs and, at any particular time, present the electorate with information about the attributes needed in new board members and provide concrete suggestions of qualified individuals. The same is true where some or all of the board members are appointed by public authorities or leaders of the parent organization. Boards that do not have formal governing responsibilities, but serve a more advisory role, can also make good use of the information in this book because the value of the decisions made and the advice provided depend to a large extent on the combination of resources available on the board. Appointing authorities may need help to see that their self-interest may be best served by heeding the recommendations provided by the governance committee.

While the governance committee is essential to building an effective board, equally important is the role of the board chair and the chief executive. Not only do they often have important contacts in the community that may lead to new board members, they shape the ongoing work of the board. Developing board meeting agendas, engaging board members in the work, and providing information are responsibilities shared by the board chair and the chief executive.

While the board building process is defined as having nine steps see page xiii, it may be useful to consider that the process has two major purposes:

1. **To replenish the board's people-power by bringing in new members**

   As outlined in Steps 1 – 4

   - Identify what the board needs.

   - Cultivate potential new members.

   - Recruit the ones that best fit the profile of what the board needs.

   - Orient them to effective service.

2. **To strengthen the board's performance**

   In Steps 5 – 9

   - Involve all members of the board.

   - Educate them about the organization.

   - Assess the board's performance.

   - Rotate responsibilities and membership.

   - Strengthen the board's morale by celebrating its accomplishments — both big and small.

GOVERNANCE COMMITTEE JOB DESCRIPTION

The governance committee is responsible for ongoing review and recommendations to enhance the quality and future viability of the board of directors. The work of the committee revolves around the following five major areas:

1. Board Roles and Responsibilities

- Leads the board in regularly reviewing and updating the board's description of its roles and areas of responsibility, and what is expected of individual board members.

2. Board Composition

- Leads in assessing current and anticipated needs related to board composition, determining the knowledge, attributes, skills, abilities, influence, and access to resources the board will need to consider in order to accomplish future work of the board.

- Develops a profile of the board as it should evolve over time.

- Identifies potential board member candidates and explores their interest and availability for board service.

- Nominates individuals to be elected as members of the board.

- In cooperation with the board chair, contacts each board member to assess his or her continuing interest in board membership and term of service and works with each board member to identify the appropriate role he or she might assume on behalf of the organization.

3. Board Knowledge

- Designs and oversees a process of board orientation, including providing information prior to election and as needed during the early stage of board service.

- Proposes and assists in implementing an ongoing program of board information and education.

4. Board Effectiveness

- Initiates periodic assessment of the board's performance. Proposes, as appropriate, changes in board structure and operations.

- Provides ongoing counsel to the board chair and other board leaders on steps they might take to enhance board effectiveness.

- Regularly reviews the board's practices regarding member participation, conflict of interest, confidentiality, etc., and suggests improvements as needed.

- Periodically reviews and updates the board's policy guidelines and practices.

5. Board Leadership

- Takes the lead in succession planning, taking steps to recruit and prepare for future board leadership.

- Nominates board members for election as board officers.

The Governance Committee Job Description is adapted from the work of Fred Miller, Chatham Group, Inc.

Good boards do not just happen: They take care, thought, and planning. Organizations with strong, active boards often spend significant time and attention on each part of the board building cycle. Good boards wanting to become great boards will continually consider how to strengthen their performance at each step of the cycle. They will ensure that everyone on the board is on the same page in terms of the board's responsibilities for the organization and their individual responsibilities as board members.

The following pages provide an outline of the roles and responsibilities of the board as a whole and for individual board members. In addition, you will find a job description for the governance committee and a summary of the nine steps involved in the board building cycle.

Included with this book is a CD-ROM containing the forms, worksheets, and sample documents presented in each of the steps. The documents are available in Microsoft® Word® and text formats and can be easily customized to suit the needs of individual boards. New to this edition of the book, the CD-ROM now includes the BoardSource board orientation tool *Presenting: Board Orientation*. This PowerPoint® program provides users with slides that can be easily customized for a board orientation session. See the Appendix on page 75 for more detailed information about the accompanying CD-ROM.

THE BOARD BUILDING CYCLE

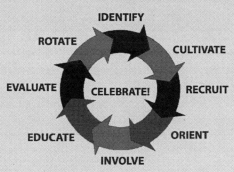

Step 1: Identify the needs of the board: the skills, knowledge, perspectives, connections, etc., needed to implement the strategic plan. What do you have? What is missing?

Step 2: Cultivate sources of potential board members and identify individuals with the desired characteristics. Ask current board members, senior staff, and others to suggest potential candidates. Find ways to connect with those candidates, get them interested in your organization, and keep them informed of your progress.

Step 3: Recruit prospects. Describe why prospective members are wanted and needed. Explain expectations and responsibilities of board members, and don't minimize requirements. Invite questions, elicit prospects' interest, and find out if they are prepared to serve.

Step 4: Orient new board members both to the organization and to the board explaining the history, programs, pressing issues, finances, facilities, bylaws, and organizational chart. Describe committees, board member responsibilities, and lists of board members and key staff members.

Step 5: Involve all board members. Discover their interests and availability. Involve them in committees or task forces. Assign them a board "buddy." Solicit feedback. Hold everyone accountable. Express appreciation for work well done.

Step 6: Educate the board. Provide information concerning your mission area. Promote exploration of issues facing the organization. Hold retreats and encourage board development activities by sending board members to seminars and workshops. Don't hide difficulties.

Step 7: Evaluate the board as a whole, as well as individual board members. Examine how the board and chief executive work as a team. Engage the board in assessing its own performance. Identify ways in which to improve. Encourage individual self-assessment.

Step 8: Rotate board members. Establish term limits. Do not automatically reelect for an additional term; consider the board's needs and the board member's performance. Explore advisability of resigning with members who are not active. Develop new leadership.

Step 9: Celebrate! Recognize victories and progress, no matter how small. Appreciate individual contributions to the board, the organization, and the community. Make room for humor and a good laugh.

Step 1: Identify

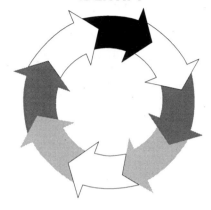

IDENTIFY

There is a need to recognize the importance of nonprofits to the vitality of the community in which they operate and to recognize the importance of effective boards to these nonprofits. Nonprofits themselves, and their boards, must assist this process by rethinking old assumptions about who should or could serve effectively on their boards and about how people can be identified, developed, and recruited.

— Benjamin R. Shute
    Corporate Secretary
    Rockefeller Brothers Fund

DEVELOP THE BOARD PROFILE

The search for new board members is a strategic activity; it has long-term implications for the board's effectiveness. It should be driven by considerations of what resources the board will need among its members in order to serve the organization well during the next few years. Having a strategic plan in place will guide the board in its choice of whom to bring onto the board. The organization's strategic direction can help to clarify the special skills and resources required on the board. For example, an organization planning to develop more of a presence on the Internet or enhance its internal technology capacities may need to recruit board members with a technology background. A symphony orchestra struggling with declining concert attendance may need board members who represent constituencies that are currently missing from the audience. Such board members may better understand the needs and interests of the audiences that are currently not being served.

What if no strategic plan or strategic framework currently exists or what if the organization is facing significant challenges and opportunities that might require a change of priorities or a change of direction? In such cases, it may be doubly important to consider the personal characteristics of potential members, such as analytical abilities or open-mindedness, as well as particular professional expertise or connections in the community.

A board profile worksheet, such as the one on pages 8–9, can assist the governance committee in developing an ideal board profile. No board is going to need everything listed on the worksheet, and many will add items that are unique to their organization and their mission. The important thing is to consider each of the major categories listed and then to develop a profile worksheet that meets the unique needs of each board.

Some of what the board will need from its members over the next several years will depend both on the organization's mission and its stage of development. The board of a five-year-old private school will have very different needs than the board of a similar school with a fifty-year-old track record. In the early years, the board will probably need members who are prepared to take on jobs that can supplement the work of a small staff, while the board of the well-established school will probably be faced with major responsibilities for fundraising. During the early years, most board members may turn out to be parents, while the mature school may realize the need for expertise and perspectives that must be found in the wider community.

IDENTIFY NECESSARY SKILLS

No matter what particular needs are dictated by the issues facing the organization, each board must look for people with leadership skills, the ability to work as part of a team, and who ask good questions and can follow through on commitments. Community involvement, political connections, and fundraising abilities will be important for most organizations. A commitment to the organization's mission and values should be a must. Professional expertise related to the organization's mission can provide important insights during strategic planning and decision making. In addition, most boards need people with financial expertise. These days, people with an understanding of information technology, entrepreneurial skills, public relations, and marketing may add value to a board's work on behalf of the organization. These professionals add value by the questions they ask, by their understanding of issues the board must deal with, and by their connections in the community. However, they should not be expected to provide their professional services to the organization.

By identifying candidates with proven leadership skills, the board ensures its pool of potential future leaders. Someone with organizational leadership experience — whether in the for-profit or nonprofit sector — may have demonstrated skills in managing groups of people, strategic planning, or finances. Not every new recruit can or should be a corporate executive; however, focusing on a prospective member's capacity for leadership can help the board to groom members for leading the board to success in the years to come.

Some organizations are required to fill a certain number of board seats with people who reflect the needs of specific geographic locations or other organizations, or who are directly affected by the organization's services. Others choose to do so because they recognize the need for the perspectives that come from different experiences and interests. A statewide organization may need board members from different parts of the state. A local social service organization may benefit from close connections to one or more religious institutions. An organization serving people with developmental disabilities may be required to have clients' family members on the board.

ADD VALUE WITH DIVERSITY

In addition to the attributes just described, each board must also seek to incorporate the different perspectives represented by individuals from different age groups and racial/ethnic groups as well as a balance of men and women. For example, increasing numbers of boards are finding it useful to include young people in their ranks because they tend to bring different assumptions to the board table. For example, their ideas about the varied use of technology tend to outstrip those of their elders. They are also less likely to feel constrained by a "we tried this already" mentality, and may, by their questions and comments, help identify "the elephant in the room." A study conducted in 2000 at the University of Wisconsin-Madison found that adults who worked with young people in making decisions about the organization reported a higher level of commitment and energy around the room.

BUILDING A START-UP BOARD

One of the first things necessary to start a nonprofit organization is to create its board. The first board has the extraordinary job of getting the organization off the ground and making it a functioning entity. This kind of board requires special people with specific skills. Individuals best suited to accomplish this big task need to

- have a strong belief in the organization's mission

- collaborate well with the founders

- be available to put the work in and have a real physical presence

- collectively possess skills in areas such as law, nonprofit accounting, project management, marketing, and communications

The first board may be tasked with helping the founders draft the initial bylaws, file IRS tax-exemption papers, incorporate the organization, plan programs, set up an office, open bank accounts, learn about their roles as board members and fiduciaries of the organization, and determine the best governance structure for their board.

It's likely that a start-up board will be comprised of people known to the founder — friends, family, and colleagues. This is natural. However, occasionally a benefactor, instrumental in funding the organization in its early stages, may ask to be included on the board — perhaps even as its chair. This could invite trouble, so consider alternative ways of incorporating the advice of benefactors that prohibits them from exercising too much influence on the decisions of the board.

In ethnically and racially diverse communities, it can be crucial that boards diversify their membership in order to respond effectively to the needs and aspirations of the community. For example, a retirement community struggling with declining enrollment might be disadvantaged by a board that does not incorporate the perspectives of the major population groups in the area. Not only does demographic diversity add depth and nuance to the board's discussions, it also serves as a symbol of the organization's values. People will consciously or unconsciously draw conclusions about what an organization stands for based on the composition of its board.

In many communities there can be a competition for "the best" board members. These people typically fall into categories such as white-collar professionals, business people, or organizational leaders. However, when considering potential board members, don't overlook individuals employed in the trades, such as carpenters and plumbers, or people in nonmanagement positions such as secretaries and technicians. The fact is that such individuals could most likely fill many of the slots on the board profile sheet and have the kind of practical minds and wisdom that would be great assets to a board.

The chief reason for developing a board that is not homogeneous is to promote exploration of a wider range of ideas and options and to reach forward-looking decisions. All organizations now operate in a very complex environment, and research has shown that systems perform best when internal diversity reflects the diversity of the environment. Boards that include men and women with different skills and professional backgrounds, ages, financial situations, and cultural and ethnic backgrounds may be better positioned to steer the organization through frequently turbulent environments than may boards where members are more homogeneous.

ROUND OUT THE BOARD

Once it is clear what kind of composition the board will need over the next several years, the governance committee must assess what characteristics and attributes its current members bring to the table. By comparing the two lists it becomes clear what gaps need to be filled in order to support the organization's strategic direction. By identifying what is needed for the future before examining the current profile, the committee is less likely to simply replicate current patterns. For example, if a well-known community leader is retiring and moving to Florida, the board may wish to fill that board spot with someone who has the same solid community leadership credentials but who is younger or possibly from a different ethnic group.

Consider the traditional "Ws" that every board depends on: Work, Wealth, and Wisdom. Every board needs people who are willing to roll up their sleeves to get things done; who have access to financial resources; and who possess the wisdom to ask the right questions, provide the needed knowledge, and support healthy discussion. Ideally, every board member should bring at least two of these attributes to the table. But there are two other Ws essential to an effective board: Wit and Witness. Humor can make it easier and more enjoyable for the board to work together, and all board members need to be able to give witness to the organization's valuable work, to tell the story so others will add their support.

The governance committee's final draft of the proposed board profile should be presented to the board for review, possible revision, and affirmation. Upon approval, the governance committee can then go to work looking for prospective new board members, not only to fill immediate vacancies, but also to meet the board's future needs over the next several years.

EXPAND BOARD DIVERSITY, BUT LIMIT BOARD SIZE

Many organizations identify their needs for inclusiveness and diversity only to confront the biggest challenge of all: how to fill all those needs without weighing down the board with too many members. Gauging the board's ideal size takes careful thought. If it is too large, some members may feel disengaged, and decision making becomes cumbersome. If the board is too small, board members may be overwhelmed and the board will not have sufficient breadth of perspective, expertise, and other resources.

The trend is toward smaller, more workable boards, but the appropriate size of any board will depend on the organization and the work the board is expected to accomplish. According to a BoardSource survey of chief executives, the size of the average board is now about 17 members. This is true among both self-perpetuating boards and boards elected by an association's membership. For example, a few years ago the board of the National Parent Teacher Association was reduced to less than a third of its original size and the board of the American Diabetes Association is in the process of reducing its membership from 56 to 31.

To maximize the board's effectiveness, all board members should represent more than one skill or attribute. For example, an environmental advocacy group identified the need for several more women, individuals younger than 40, someone with financial expertise, someone knowledgeable about environmental politics, and people with leadership potential. Armed with this list, the governance committee's search resulted in a slate that included two women: one a thirty-year-old female CPA with a personal commitment to the organization's cause and policy know-how; the other a thirty-six-year-old up-and-coming community leader with independent financial resources and political connections. A nursing home board let it be known that it was going to need members with financial expertise, connections to the local African American community, and understanding of issues facing frail, elderly people. As a result, the staff identified a promising prospect in an African American man who served as chief financial officer of a major community development organization. His father was a former resident.

Another way to expand the resources available to the board is to use advisory councils: groups of people who agree to make themselves available by providing consultation pro bono. However, it is usually best not to call them advisory "boards." Calling them "councils" defines their role better and avoids confusion with the board of directors. Advisory councils may not even have to meet as a whole, but be available as individuals when the need arises. They can also be a stepping stone to board membership — a good way for potential members to get to know the organization and for the board to see if they are right for board service. An organization may establish a number of advisory councils. For example, a local public television station might create a council made up of young parents, another of cultural aficionados, and another to support the station's fundraising effort.

North American organizations that do work elsewhere in the world may want to include board members from the regions being served; however, there are implications associated with worldwide board participation. Consider the costs involved with recruiting and involving these members. Will they be flown in to attend meetings or will the organization need to invest in video conferencing technologies? Will they have the ability to fully participate on the board and committees? One approach to this dilemma may be to look for individuals within North America with connections in those regions who could appropriately fill that role. However, if the organization is international in scope (not just a North American organization with programs abroad), then it should have international representation.

BOARD PROFILE WORKSHEET

EXPERTISE/SKILLS/PERSONAL DATA

The worksheet on page 8 can be adapted by organizations to assess their current board composition and plan for the future. The governance committee can develop an appropriate grid for the organization and then present its recommendations to the full board.

In considering board building, an organization is legally obligated to follow its bylaws, which may include specific criteria on board size, structure, and composition. Or the bylaws may need to be updated to incorporate and acknowledge changes in the environment and community that made board structure changes necessary or desirable.

Remember, an organization will look for different skills and strengths from its board members depending on its stage of development and other circumstances.

STEP 1: ACTION STEPS

- Annually review the organization's mission and strategic direction in order to identify the needs of the board better.

- Carefully consider the diversity of intellectual, social, financial, demographic, and reputational resources needed on the board.

- Develop a profile of characteristics needed on the board and compare it with what is currently available among its members.

- Ensure diversity of backgrounds, knowledge, and other resources — without becoming too big — by looking for members who represent more than one desired characteristic.

BOARD PROFILE WORKSHEET

	Current Members						Prospective Members					
	1	2	3	4	5	6	A	B	C	D	E	F
Age												
Under 18												
19 – 34												
35 – 50												
51 – 65												
Over 65												
Gender												
Male												
Female												
Race/Ethnicity												
African American/Black												
Asian/Pacific Islander												
Caucasian												
Hispanic/Latino												
Native American/Indian												
Other												
Resources												
Money to give												
Access to money												
Access to other resources (foundations, corporate support)												
Availability for active participation solicitation visits, grant writing												
Community Connections												
Religious organizations												
Corporate												
Education												
Media												
Political												
Philanthropy												
Small business												
Social services												
Other												

BOARD PROFILE WORKSHEET

	Current Members						Prospective Members					
	1	**2**	**3**	**4**	**5**	**6**	**A**	**B**	**C**	**D**	**E**	**F**
Qualities												
Leadership skills/Motivator												
Willingness to work/Availability												
Personal connection with the organization's mission												
Personal Style												
Consensus builder												
Good communicator												
Strategist												
Visionary												
Bridge builder												
Areas of Expertise												
Administration/Management												
Entrepreneurship												
Financial management												
Accounting												
Investments												
Fundraising												
Government												
Law												
Marketing, public relations												
Human resources												
Strategic planning												
Physical plant (architect, engineer)												
Real estate												
Representative of clients												
Special program focus (e.g., education, health, public policy, social services)												
Technology												
Other												
Number of years (or terms) on the board												

Step 2: Cultivate

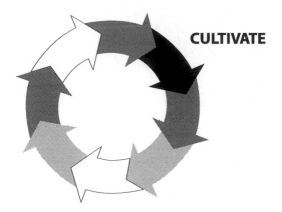

CULTIVATE

Teamwork is the ability to work together toward a common vision, the ability to direct individual accomplishments toward organizational objectives. It is the fuel that allows common people to attain uncommon results.

— Andrew Carnegie
    1835 – 1919 Philanthr   opist

DEVELOP A POOL OF POTENTIAL BOARD MEMBERS

Identifying relates to the board's needs. Cultivating, on the other hand, is all about the prospects and candidates. Cultivating potential board members should be an ongoing activity. When the time comes to nominate new board members, it is useful to have a pool of people to choose from. Because board membership requires a significant investment of personal time and energy, it is important to find candidates who care deeply about the organization's mission and who have what it takes to be an effective board member.

Cultivation involves both 1) creating a pool of individuals who might in the future be asked to stand for election to the board and, 2) developing the kind of relationships with them that will either lead to board membership or some other form of supportive relationship. This means finding them, getting them informed about the organization's work, and getting them interested in becoming involved. It is, in some ways, like "dating" in personal relationships — the process of getting to know each other. All dates do not end in marriage. Some become good friends; others drop off the screen. Without a period of dating, wrong matches are often made, even when it appears to be "love at first sight." The outcome of the cultivation process should increase the likelihood that someone with the right qualifications will be waiting in the wings when the need arises.

The governance committee manages the cultivation process, making sure that the entire board is involved and that everyone understands how best to participate. The board should be aware of the characteristics and qualities needed in potential board members. It is crucial for board members to know what they should or shouldn't do when dealing with someone who may be a potential board member. For example, no one should ask potential candidates if they want to serve on the board; the governance committee is responsible for delegating that task. On the other hand, board members ought to feel free to share information about the organization's work, invite people to events, and discover their levels of support for the mission. The governance committee should collect information about individuals who might become likely candidates, maintain a prospects file, and take next steps, if appropriate.

INVOLVE EVERYONE IN THE PROCESS

Recruitment is a team effort and should involve more than the board members and the chief executive. Senior staff and former board members should also be expected to introduce prospective candidates to the organization, and major donors could be asked to think of people who might be interested in board service. Professionals in related fields as well as other colleagues and board members of other nonprofit groups may be good referral sources. Also inquire with local religious institutions and volunteer clearinghouses. Organizations that have a good relationship with a funder might find some good leads there as well.

A good example of how to involve board members in the process of identifying potential board members was provided by BoardSource consultant Katha Kissman who told of a "Rolodex® party." This informal party was organized at a board member's home and required board members to bring their address books or Rolodexes® with them. As they flipped through their lists, they talked briefly about the people they thought might be a good fit. Some people surprised themselves by suddenly remembering someone they had not even considered but who might be a good candidate. Others identified individuals who might not be available for the board, but who might be cultivated for other kinds of support. The party had important side benefits as well: The board members had fun and got a chance to get to know one another better.

The chief executive's role in cultivation may vary widely depending on the organization. Regardless, the chief executive should be involved in the cultivation process because he or she must develop and sustain strong working relationships with board members. The chief executive will also have important contacts in the community that could lead to potential board members. However, in no way should the chief executive be the only person responsible for identifying prospective board members. If a board lets this happen, the organization's credibility could be at stake. In cases where the chief executive is seen as hand-picking the board, the community might wonder whether organizational accountability is compromised.

CAST A WIDE NET

But the board also needs to look beyond its usual peripheral view of board prospects. For instance, a health-related charity might look for leads among medical professionals, social workers, clergy, and family members of people who have benefited from the organization's services. A local Boys and Girls Club board might develop relationships with recent graduates who have exhibited strong leadership abilities. A cultural organization might do well by cross-referencing season subscribers with substantial contributors. An institution with nationwide affiliates might need to seek advice and referrals from people in each region of the country.

Keep an eye on the local media for stories of people who are active in the community or who have shown an interest related to the organization's mission. Contact universities with programs in nonprofit management or with graduate programs in fields related to the institution's mission and ask for suggestions of faculty, staff, graduates, and students. Membership associations could be fertile ground for some charity boards. For example, a nonprofit that helps children with learning disabilities could tap a teachers association for suggestions.

Consider people with a vested interest in the work of the organization. Local business owners might jump at the chance to serve on a board that would benefit the immediate community — perhaps a group that provides after-school activities for youth with the goal of cutting down on vandalism and other crimes. A college or university may look to its alumni or parents. Any large institution might find potential candidates with good track records from among those serving on the organization's special committees. Local leadership programs can be excellent sources of individuals looking for opportunities to get involved at the leadership level in community organizations. In addition, numerous corporations have board placement programs for their employees and may be on the lookout for nonprofit boards in need of members.

To help develop more inclusive boards, some United Ways have offered a program called Project Blueprint, which aims to prepare African Americans, Hispanics, Asian/Pacific Islanders, and Native Americans for board membership. The program requires that graduates spend at least one term on the board of a United Way charity, but some local United Way officials may be willing to refer former trainees, who have served their required terms, for service on other boards. Religious institutions and ethnically identified professional associations, such as the Latino/Hispanic Chamber of Commerce or the Asian American Small Business Association, may also be good sources of potential board members with roots and connections in particular ethnic communities.

An organization may also choose to advertise or otherwise announce that the board is looking for individuals interested in board service. Board service opportunities can be listed in newspapers, posted on the organization's lobby bulletin board or Web site, and listed on Web sites that offer to match interested people with boards seeking members (e.g., www.boardnetusa.org or www.volunteermatch.org). This approach can serve to introduce new constituencies to the board, but it must be used with care to avoid creating misunderstandings and feelings of rejection or elitism in cases where somebody offers to serve but is not chosen. Board vacancy announcements should convey brief information about the organization, the responsibilities of the board, and the characteristics the board is looking for in a board member. When people express interest, they should receive more specific information about the responsibilities of board members as well as an application form (for more information, see Prospective Board Member Information Sheet on page 17). The receipt of applications should be acknowledged and applicants should be informed of the next steps. It is very important to communicate that the selection of board members is based on a combination of factors determined by the board and that not being selected for board service is not perceived as a negative reflection on a person's qualifications. At this time other opportunities for volunteer service should also be presented.

Holding occasional open houses or special events for people expressing interest in the organization's work is yet another way to identify potential board members. Make sure key board members are present to meet and mingle with the guests, that information is provided in concise and attractive ways, and that there are plenty of opportunities for people to ask questions and interact. Information should be collected from each guest so the appropriate party, whether at the board level or the staff level, will be able to follow up.

There are some nonprofit organizations, such as religious institutions, community associations, and clubs, that are permitted to look exclusively within their own membership for board members and are not required to seek members from outside. In most of these cases, membership or home ownership (in the case of community association boards) may be a requirement to board service. Even though these boards are not held to the same broad representational requirements, it is still wise to make sure that board members possess the diversity of skills and personal characteristics necessary for an effectively run board.

CULTIVATE RELATIONSHIPS

Once prospects have been identified, the next step is to develop a relationship between the prospect and the organization. Create a file for each individual or complete a Prospective Board Member Information Sheet, such as the one found on page 17. The information gathered on each prospect should include the person's contact information, special interests, other board service, professional affiliations, and the name of the person referring this individual, along with other relevant information. Make sure the files are updated when an individual's information changes. The files should be maintained by the governance committee and may be kept in the chief executive's office or some other place with restricted access in order to safeguard private information. When the time comes to identify candidates for the next election, the committee will have a ready resource.

As soon as prospective candidates are identified, begin to bring them into the fold. Let them know that you would like them to get to know the organization. Send them annual reports, brochures, newsletters, and other basic information. When the organization gets a favorable mention in the press, send them clippings along with a brief handwritten note. Invite them to special events and ask if they would like to observe the organization's programs.

Invite potential board members to serve on a committee or a task force, or to participate in other volunteer activities. Some organizations require that prospective board members serve in some volunteer capacity for as much as a year before they are invited to join. As they become more familiar with the institution and the board, it may become apparent that they have additional skills or interests that could benefit the organization, or it may turn out that they would not be the right match for the board.

Don't dismiss people who serve on other boards or whose schedules would not allow them to join the board right away. It could be months, or even years, before they are ready. Keep in mind that the more boards people serve on, or the more irons they have in the fire, the less time they will likely have to devote to the work of your board. So be prepared to wait and keep them on the prospect list. The important thing is to keep in touch and keep them updated on the organization's activities and achievements.

PRACTICE DIPLOMACY

Avoid misunderstandings by being clear with prospects that not everyone who is invited to take an active interest in the organization's work — including the possibility of board service at some point in the future — will end up as a board member. If someone seems to meet some of the criteria listed in the desired profile, it may be wise to say that the governance committee might be interested in talking with them at some point about possible board service and ask if this would be of interest to them. Let them know that the committee considers a variety of factors, including getting the right mix of talents, perspectives, and experiences on the board.

As stated earlier, the cultivation process will not necessarily lead to board membership. While getting to know individuals in the prospect pool, it is important to take note of behaviors that indicate whether they would serve the board well. Are they inquisitive? Do they care about the mission? Do they follow through on commitments? Do they listen? The board profile will provide guidance in developing the prospect pool, but remember that while the board needs a diversity of perspectives and backgrounds around the board table, it also requires individuals who are able to understand and accept the perspectives of those who differ from them.

One word of caution: When looking for prospective board members, sometimes the names of a husband and wife team, or others who share a close personal relationship, will be suggested. Often couples are interested in the same things and will get involved in the same causes. While it is smart to keep both persons in mind for the future, it is generally not a good idea to have couples serve on a board at the same time — particularly on a small board. They may personally feel that they can think independently and make their own decisions, but there is a potential for their board colleagues to view them as holding a voting block or feel uncomfortable if they were to disagree with each other during contentious discussions. The one who is not the best match for the board profile at a particular time might be cultivated for a different volunteer role in the organization or kept in mind for a later time.

In family foundations, it is customary and accepted that several members of the board will come from the family. The objective is to ensure that the wishes of the founder are respected or that the distribution of funds continues to meet family members' consensus. However, even family foundation boards benefit from the wisdom and detachment of some independent minds.

So long as the board has clearly documented its needs, selection criteria, and its process for recruiting and nominating new board members, it is in a better position to protect itself from accusations of unfair discrimination. Because board service does not involve an employment contract, there is generally no legal recourse that can be taken. An organization can still be open to public criticism if disgruntled constituents sense that the selection process was unfair or unbalanced.

At times there is little distinction between the work done during the cultivation step and the recruitment step in the board building cycle. The cultivation period should be a time not only to develop a pool of prospective board members, but also to begin to narrow down the choice candidates so when the board is ready to bring on a new member, the process is ready to deliver.

STEP 2: ACTION STEPS

- Continually develop a pool of potential board members.

- Identify sources of individuals with the characteristics described in the board profile.

- Cast a wide net and look at nontraditional sources for prospects.

- Involve a wide range of people in the cultivation process, including board, senior staff, major donors, and other constituents.

- Cultivate relationships with individuals who seem promising.

- Invite prospects to participate in some way in support of the organization.

- Keep records of individuals who might be potential board candidates in the future.

HOW AND WHERE TO FIND BOARD MEMBERS

Where to find suggestions of good board members

- Colleagues
- Board members of other nonprofits
- Articles and reports in the local media
- Chief executive and other senior staff
- Board members
- Volunteer centers
- Local leadership programs
- Current volunteers
- Current advisory council members or task force members
- Other ideas?

Whom to consider for board membership

- Community leaders
- Executives of local or national corporations, including those not at a senior level
- Owners of small businesses
- Individuals in professions related to the organization's mission
- Current and prospective major donors
- People who have benefited from the organization's services, or their relatives
- Current or past volunteers (where applicable)
- People who have an affinity with the mission
- Other ideas?

Where to look for prospective board members

- Religious institutions and congregations
- Major corporations' outreach programs
- Trade, professional, and fraternal associations
- Local businesses
- Organizations representing various racial and ethnic groups
- Local colleges and universities, community colleges
- Electronic databases (www.guidestar.org, www.boardnetusa.org)
- Hobby centers, clubs, community centers
- Other ideas?

PROSPECTIVE BOARD MEMBER INFORMATION SHEET

Name of prospective board member: _____

Title: _____

Organization: _____

Address: _____

City: _____ State: _____ ZIP: _____

Daytime Phone: _____ Evening Phone: _____

Mobile Phone: _____ E-mail: _____

Source of referral/information: _____

Special skills

☐ Fundraising   ☐ Marketing/Public Relations

☐ Personnel/Human Resources   ☐ Technology

☐ Finances   ☐ Legal

☐ Business   ☐ Other: _____

Professional background

☐ For-profit business   ☐ Nonprofit organization

☐ Government   ☐ Other: _____

Education

☐ Some high school   ☐ Some graduate coursework

☐ High school graduate   ☐ Graduate degree

☐ Some college   ☐ Other: _____

☐ Undergraduate college degree

Other affiliations: _____

Other board service: _____

Known levels of giving: _____

Other pertinent information: _____

Step 3: Recruit

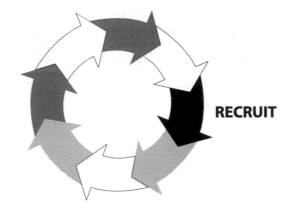

RECRUIT

We look for committed people who are willing to invest their time helping us achieve our mission.

— Rita Battello
    Board Chair
    The Guadelupe Center, Kansas City

EXPLORE INTEREST AND MUTUAL FIT

The recruitment portion of the board building cycle is a highly personal activity — and a two-way street. It is a process of actively exploring the interest in possible board membership with potential candidates. This is a prospect's opportunity to learn about the organization and the board and to find out what the expectations are of board membership. But it also gives current board members a chance to gauge prospects' interest and determine whether they are right for service on this board at this time.

Recruitment is a three-step process.

- The first step is a general exploration of the prospect's interest in board service. What is the person's interest in the mission area? Does the board present a good fit for this individual? Are there constraints that would prevent him or her from fully participating on the board?

- The second step is to elicit possible commitment to serve if elected.

- Step three is the process of nomination and election.

To aid in the recruitment process, particularly if a number of potential candidates are to be interviewed, many boards use a rating sheet outlining key issues that will help compare candidate qualifications and assist in developing the final slate. The issues listed on the rating sheet should be reviewed before each election since particular needs may change from year to year. For example, one year a board was faced with the sudden resignation of its lone technology "guru" because of illness. Because the board would have to make a substantial investment in new technological systems in the near future, finding someone with a technology background became urgent. Another year other specific issues might rise to the top of the list, but never would a single characteristic be sufficient to elect someone to the board. Demographic diversity and personal qualities must also be considered. A sample Board Candidate Rating Form is provided on page 21.

ENGAGE THE PROSPECTS

The first step in the process might be delegated to a couple of people from the governance committee or to a board member who seems appropriately matched to a particular candidate. If the chief executive will be involved, it is beneficial to have a board member also be part of the interview team.

The following are some suggestions for how to approach the first part of the recruitment process.

- First, review the information that is available about the candidate prior to having an exploratory conversation, then contact the candidate to set up a meeting time. During this meeting, let the candidate know that:

  - the board will need to fill a number of seats over the next couple of years;

  - he or she has been suggested as a person who might have a great deal to offer; and that

  - you are acting on behalf of the board to explore interest and availability for board service with a number of people before a slate is put together.

- During the meeting provide a brief description of the organization, its mission, its services, and its strategic direction. Bring brief, up-to-date materials to leave with candidates for their review at a later date or to prompt questions on the spot. If the person has been involved as a committee or task force member, a volunteer or a financial supporter, affirm their previous knowledge and tailor the description accordingly. Be sure to invite their questions about the organization and find out how the candidate feels about your organization's mission, its work, and its reputation.

- Describe in general terms the roles and responsibilities of the board and what is expected of board members. Again, invite their questions about board service and find out if they would be interested in having their name presented to the governance committee as a possible board candidate. If so, determine whether there are any constraints in terms of their participation (e.g. conflicts of interest, commitment to other boards, etc.).

- If candidates have not already been involved in the organization's work, this would be a good time to invite them to participate in a project or on a task force. The recruitment period provides an opportunity to get a sense of how dedicated and effective candidates would be if chosen for the board. Many organizations try to involve potential board candidates in some of the organization's hands-on activities, such as helping to build a house or cleaning up the shoreline along a polluted river. By rolling up their sleeves and volunteering, it gives them a more intimate understanding of what the organization is all about and demonstrates to current board members a genuine desire to serve. Ideally some of this is happening during the cultivation period, but may not happen until the conversation about board service turns serious.

EVALUATE THE PROSPECTS

After each interview, prepare a report for the governance committee summarizing what you learned, raising any red flags, and concluding with a general rating of the candidate as a potential board member, or complete the rating schedule if the governance committee has provided one. If the person did not ask questions about the organization or about the board, he or she might not be a promising board candidate since one of the important responsibilities of a board member is to ask questions.

Questions concerning time for committee work or comments about a heavy travel schedule might raise red flags concerning the person's availability for active board participation. This may also be relevant for celebrity/well-known persons. If they are unlikely to be able or willing to participate in the work of the board on a regular basis, it may be wiser to design a special support role for them rather than elect them to the board.

As part of narrowing down the list of prospective candidates, it is often a good idea to do some confidential research about them. This can provide valuable information about their past performance on boards, the extent of their expertise, and their willingness to be a team player. These days, background checks are routinely used when hiring a new employee. It may be equally important when selecting members of the board, which, after all, is the group that is expected to assure the public that the organization is in good hands. This usually means that board members ought to have a clean legal slate as well as a good reputation in the community and the ability to carry out their duties. If board members will be expected to provide financial support, it might be helpful to check the latest annual report from other organizations on whose board the person has served to see what kinds of gifts he or she has given. However, not all organizations publish their lists of donors, and a gift to one organization does not guarantee a gift to another. In any case, it might be disappointing to elect a well-to-do person to the board with the assumption of a generous contribution only to find out that he or she does not engage in philanthropy.

Take a good look at the culture of the board and be truthful about the kinds of members the board is looking for. A board that finds itself falling into repetitive cycles may talk about getting someone who will "mix things up." However, the reality is that someone could shake things up a bit too much and either become ostracized from the board or challenge the board so much that it ultimately fractures. Therefore, take care when discussing board service with prospects who do not fit the mold of the traditional board member.

BOARD CANDIDATE RATING FORM

Name of candidate:_____

Name of rater:_____

Interviewed by:_____

Date of interview:_____

On a scale of 1 – 5 (1=not acceptable, 5=great), please rate the candidate on each item listed below.

		Rating
1.	Proven interest in our mission	
2.	Knowledge and understanding of our work	
3.	Professional knowledge and skills needed by the board (technology, statistics, health policy)	
4.	Connections in the community (media, politics, health care)	
5.	Fundraising experience and willingness to participate	
6.	Ability to make a substantial financial contribution	
7.	Experience in working with people from other ethnic backgrounds	
8.	Ability to listen well	
9.	Ability to express ideas and opinions clearly	
10.	Ability to participate effectively in a conversation neither monopolizing nor hanging back	
11.	Sense of humor, positive presence	
12.	Ability to ask appropriate questions	
13.	Ability to participate on a regular basis in the board's work	
	TOTAL	

Other strong points:

Red flags:

Prepare for Nomination and Election

The second phase of the recruitment strategy begins once the governance committee has identified a group of viable and interested candidates. It is now time to determine the final slate of nominees to be presented to the board, the membership, or the appointing authorities. The chief executive will usually participate in the deliberations and have a voice, but not necessarily a determining voice, in the selection of nominees. Some organizations seek to have more than one candidate for each open position; in others, the board prefers to be presented with just one nominee per position. If the bylaws stipulate one way or the other, the bylaws must be followed.

In preparation for board elections or new appointments, the governance committee should start by looking at who is leaving the board and who is eligible for re-election (or re-appointment) to a new term. Make sure that everyone who is eligible for re-election is carefully evaluated both in terms of the needs of the board (as spelled out in the board profile) and in terms of the person's past performance. Ask each board member who expresses an interest in serving another term to submit a completed self-evaluation to assist the governance committee in preparing the new slate (an example of a board member self-evaluation is found on page 61). If a letter of agreement was signed at the beginning of a board member's term, this may be the time for the member to review the letter with the chair and reflect on whether they believe the board member upheld that agreement.

Re-election to the board should not be automatic. If the board profile grid indicates that the board needs someone with very different qualifications, the governance committee might recommend against renominating a current member in favor of bringing on someone with much needed expertise. For example, an organization faced with building a new facility for its services might add someone with solid knowledge of real estate and construction issues. In these situations, the committee must act with care and compassion toward the person not being renominated and share its reasoning with the full board. Circumstances like these have no easy answers, and each situation must be handled differently.

Interview the Candidates

As a final step before formally nominating someone for the board, it is wise for the board chair, the chair of the governance committee, and/or the chief executive to have a talk with the person. In order to make sure that candidates are fully aware of what board membership in this organization entails, here are important things to cover:

- Let candidates know why they are invited to stand for election. Is it because they work in the technology industry? Because of their corporate contacts? Because of a personal quality such as being known as a consensus builder? If they are representative of people served by the organization, are they known for asking good questions or having a particularly good understanding of the issues facing the organization's customers? Present them with a board member job description or the letter of agreement that new board members are asked to sign, and discuss any specific expectations, such as levels of financial contribution and involvement in fundraising or providing professional advice related to board decisions.

- During discussions about personal financial contribution and fundraising, some candidates may balk at the thought of asking friends for gifts. Hear them out, but remind them that asking for donations is a small part of fundraising — and often not a necessary role for every board member. Cultivating donors, telling them about the organization, keeping them updated on its activities, and sending hand-written notes to thank them for their interest is all some board members may need to do to help bring in generous gifts. The actual request for money may come from the board chair, other board members, or the chief executive. It is important for potential board members to understand that for organizations that solicit contributions, every board member should be a donor, no matter the amount of the gift — though it helps to have a few board members who have access to substantial financial resources. Some funders now make a point of asking if all board members contribute financially. One hundred percent participation shows that the board is committed to the organization.

- Ensure that they know how often the board meets and what is expected concerning meeting attendance and committee work. Give them a general sense of how much time will be required and provide them with a schedule of board and committee meetings. What if the board always meets in the evening on the first Tuesday of the month and the candidate has a standing teaching commitment at that time? Better to find out now rather than after the election.

- Ask potential nominees about the other boards on which they serve and whether they'd be overcommitted if they joined another board. Some board members like to ask where their organization stands on a candidate's list of charitable priorities. Being too far from the top is a good indication that he or she might not be able to commit the time or resources expected of board members.

- Explore a candidate's reasons for wanting to join the board. To understand what might motivate candidates, consider the things about the organization that persuaded current members to join. Was it the chance to help shape a new program? To develop fundraising skills? To keep a hand in a lifelong professional interest after retirement? To give back to the community? To be part of a group that is accomplishing something important? Or mostly for the camaraderie?

Some people are flattered just to be asked. Some people join boards in gratitude for an organization that helped a loved one. Being a board member of certain organizations can bestow prestige and facilitate professional contacts. There is nothing wrong with any of these motivations, as long as the individual also supports the mission and is prepared to actively participate in the work of the board.

If potential nominees have not yet had an opportunity to be involved with the organization's work, encourage them to visit and, if appropriate, to observe programs and services in action. Meeting current board members and key staff, and possibly some of the constituents, can also help candidates reach a decision about whether this is for them. Sitting in on a board meeting or two might do the same thing.

Beware of Red Flags

When interviewing candidates during the recruitment process, be aware of the "red flags" that could cause trouble down the road. It is advisable to exercise caution with people

- who are trying to pad a resume or enhance their position in the community without actually expecting to do much work or who expect to be deferred to because of their celebrity status

- who bring a personal agenda to the board such as the music lover bent on making the orchestra play more pop music, the health center patient who is intent on fixing the clinic's scheduling problems, or the political activist committed to changing the organization's approach and values

- who present themselves as champions of "what is just and right," as such people often fail to hear or respect what others are saying and have a way of driving other board members away

Surprisingly, caution may also need to be exercised when encountering individuals with previous board experience. While such experience in general is a plus, it can be a negative if they assume that they already know how things should be done even though they do not yet understand the history and culture of this particular board and organization.

Appointing potential board candidates to a committee or task force may provide a better sense of whether they are team players or lone wolves. Keep in mind that the power of a board is collective teamwork. Too many lone wolves — no matter how bright and enterprising — can stand in the way of consensus building and prevent the board from getting its work done. A diversity of opinions and ideas is crucial, but the board must eventually come to a collective decision.

Be honest throughout the process of recruiting new board members. Organizations occasionally go all out to recruit someone who is prominent in the community or who has financial resources. In doing so, they may paint too rosy a picture to lure a candidate onto the board — a tactic that can backfire. Not being completely forthcoming about what is involved in board membership can result in a hasty and embarrassing resignation. Similarly, inviting an individual with financial resources to sit on a board with a promise that he or she won't have to do any work or even attend meetings can create resentment among other board members — with no guarantee that those financial resources will end up in the organization's coffers. It is wise to keep in mind that when a board asks little of its members or its potential members, that is usually what it gets.

Close the Deal

Assuming the interview revealed no negative or worrisome information, before concluding, ask potential candidates if they would be willing to serve if nominated and elected, and encourage them to make a thoughtful and informed decision. People who are overly ambitious — or feeling pressured — may join but soon find themselves pressed for time and money — particularly if they are asked to make substantial financial contributions to more than one organization.

If a candidate expresses willingness to serve, let the candidate know when the election is expected to take place and how he or she will be notified of the outcome. Mention the board orientation process and ask the candidate to pencil in the time scheduled for the orientation session on his or her calendar and make it clear that all

MOTIVATION AND BOARDS

Why do board members volunteer their time, treasure, and talent? Board membership is — and should be — a significant commitment on the part of busy individuals. Before embarking on board recruitment and measures to keep current board members involved, board and staff need to understand and appreciate some of the underlying motivations behind board service.

MOTIVES THAT LEAD INDIVIDUALS TO JOIN BOARDS

- Altruism and a concern for the public good
- Community status and/or public visibility and recognition
- Altruistic business interests
- Prestige — affiliation adding to stature, socially, professionally, or otherwise
- Pressure from others personal or business and reluctance to say no for fear of negative repercussions
- To "get in there and get things done"
- Counter other people's perceptions of one's self
- Desire to learn
- Desire for meaning in one's life
- Desire for power

MOTIVES THAT LEAD BOARDS TO DETERMINE INDIVIDUALS FOR MEMBERSHIP

- Immediate recognition by the public (providing a form of advertising)
- Politics
- Need for greater representation or wider perspectives (gender, race, age, geography, profession, etc.)
- Commitment to "the cause" (e.g., children, the environment, the arts)
- Integrity, intelligence, courage to act

Adapted from *Directors and Trustees, A Candid Assessment of Their Motivation and Performance* by Nils Yngve Wessell, Vantage Press, 1998.

MATERIALS TO SHARE WITH POTENTIAL BOARD MEMBERS

- Annual reports

- Brochures

- Board rosters

- Newsletters

- Publications and programs list

- The organization's Web site address

- Schedule of board meetings

- Annual calendar

- Roles and responsibilities of the board

- Roles and responsibilities of individual board members

- Brief written history or fact sheet on the organization

- Current case statement

- Committee job descriptions

- Schedules of committee meetings

- Recent press clippings

new board members are required to go through board orientation to ensure that they will quickly be able to become an active participant in the work of the board.

If a candidate declines the invitation to stand for election to the board, thank the person for considering the possibility and ask if he or she might be willing to be considered again in the future. For example, if candidates are currently on other boards, they might be willing to join when their term is up. Whether the answer is yes or no, keep the door open and continue to cultivate their interest in the organization. Even candidates who decline board membership altogether may become regular donors or decide later on to become involved in another capacity.

APPOINTED AND MEMBER-ELECTED BOARDS

In associations where the members elect the board, and in organizations where an external authority appoints members to the board, the governance committee's responsibilities in the recruitment and nominations process include the following:

- Identify the skills, perspectives, and personal qualities needed on the board at any particular time and make these known to the membership or the appointing authority.

- Invite nominations in accordance with the criteria spelled out.

- Explore with nominees their understanding of board member responsibilities and what is expected of them in terms of participation. Remind them that as members of the board they will share responsibility for the whole organization and its mission and that their concern must not be only be a particular segment of the constituency.

- Find out if nominees would be able and willing to serve.

- From those nominated and interviewed, develop a slate of the individuals that best responds to the organization's and the board's needs.

- Present the slate along with each person's qualifications. When more than one name is presented for each position, it is often a good idea to make the electorate aware of the composition of the rest of the board. This may assist in electing a well-balanced board.

- Point out to the electorate or the appointing authorities that their self-interest is tied to having a board composed of people who together will support organizational excellence. This means that to be an effective leadership body, the board needs individuals who are able to think strategically about the whole organization, not narrowly about any particular segment.

For membership organizations, the governance committee plays a pivotal role between the membership, the board, and prospective board members. Because membership — not the existing board members — elects new board members, the committee needs to present a fair picture of all the candidates and how they fit into the needs of the board. The committee should communicate to the membership that, once the board has been elected, the board must be trusted to keep the best interests of the membership in mind as it does its work. Constant questioning and second-guessing of board decisions should not be necessary.

FORMAL NOMINATION AND ELECTION

The final phase in the recruitment process is for the governance committee to present the slate of candidates to the board or to the appointing or electing body. Membership associations hopefully have clearly spelled out election procedures. Self-perpetuating boards sometimes do not. To prepare the board for voting, distribute information about the names on the slate to the board prior to election. It is not appropriate to have nominees present in the boardroom during the election since board members should feel free to raise questions about a nominee or to share recent information that might be relevant. To avoid possible awkwardness, any discussion of nominees should be conducted in executive session prior to the formal election, which should be held in open meeting, whether by voice vote or by written ballot, and the results recorded in the minutes.

For boards with current board members up for re-election, having those members in the boardroom during the vote might introduce some confusion and tension. It might be wise for boards to develop a written policy for these circumstances or to request candidates to leave the room during election. The policy may state that when current members are up for re-election, all voting is done by written ballots instead of a voice vote.

While some boards prefer the governance committee to present a preselected slate of candidates that have been properly vetted, this may have the appearance of the governance committee controlling the election, not the board as a whole. Other boards may prefer that the board have more influence over the final slate and ask the governance committee to present more than one candidate per slot, thus allowing the board to make its final determination. A respected, carefully composed governance committee should earn the trust of peers to create the right slate or proposing the right candidates for board confirmation. Whichever procedure a board chooses to follow should be clearly outlined in its bylaws or policies.

As soon as the board elects its new members, the board chair should contact the newly elected to welcome them. This may be done by phone, but to emphasize the importance of the role they are accepting, the candidates should be informed in writing about their election to the board and asked to indicate their acceptance in writing. Some boards now ask board members to sign a formal agreement that outlines the mutual expectations between the board and its members. Some may also include an official swearing-in ceremony when new members attend their first board meeting, at which time they pledge their service to the organization and its mission and formally acknowledge their responsibilities as board members.

Along with a warm "welcome aboard," new members should be reminded of the upcoming board orientation session which is hopefully already designed and organized.

SAMPLE BOARD MEMBER LETTER OF AGREEMENT

As a board member of the XYZ, I am fully committed to the mission and have pledged to help carry it out. I understand that my duties and responsibilities include the following:

1. I will be fiscally responsible, with other board members, for this organization. I will know what our budget is and take an active part in reviewing, approving, and monitoring the budget.

2. I know my legal responsibilities for this organization as a member of the board and will take an active part in establishing and overseeing the organization's policies and programs.

3. I will act in accordance with the bylaws and operating principles outlined in the manual and understand that I am morally responsible, as a member of the board, for the health and well-being of this organization.

4. I will give what is for me a substantial annual financial donation.

5. I will actively participate in fundraising in whatever ways are best suited for me and agreed on with those in charge of the organization's fundraising. These may include individual solicitations, undertaking special events, writing mail appeals, and the like. I am making a good faith agreement to do my best and to help raise as much money as I can.

6. I will actively promote XYZ in the community and will encourage and support its staff.

7. I will prepare for and attend board meetings, be available for phone consultation, and serve on at least one committee, as needed.

8. If I am not able to meet my obligations as a board member, I will offer my resignation.

9. In signing this document, I understand that no quotas are being set and that no rigid standards of measurement and achievement are being formed, and trust that all board members will carry out the above agreements to the best of our ability.

Signed:_____ Date:_____
                        BOARD MEMBER

Received by:_____ Date:_____
                        BOARD CHAIR

STEP 3: ACTION STEPS

- Explore the interest of potential board members by engaging them in conversation or involving them in the organization's activities.

- Evaluate the prospects to ensure a right fit for the board and organization.

- Commission the governance committee with identifying a slate of candidates.

- Conduct personal interviews with candidates and gauge their willingness to serve on the board if nominated.

- Steer clear of overcommitted candidates who may not be able to commit the necessary time or money.

- Make sure the board has sufficient information on each nominee prior to holding elections.

- Ensure that an overall consensus exists on the election process.

Step 4: Orient

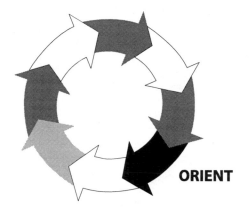

ORIENT

Board members don't always have an intuitive mystique or skills to do the job. If this is important work, then proper training must be done.

— Elaine Jacobson
Board Member
Planned Parenthood of Southern Arizona

I believe good board orientation and continuing leadership development opportunities for board members responsible for governance help avoid most troublesome situations and behaviors.

— Frances Hesselbein
Chairman
Leader to Leader Institute, New York, NY

PREPARE NEW MEMBERS FOR ACTIVE PARTICIPATION

Orientation actually begins before someone is asked to join the board. It starts when that person is first approached about the possibility of serving; or, for membership organizations that nominate and elect board members, it begins before potential board members decide to put their name in the hopper. The formal orientation is a continuation of that process. Ideally, orientation should be held before new board members attend their first board meeting and should be organized by the governance committee with the chief executive and the board chair.

Each organization needs to determine how best to ensure that all new board members learn what they need to know as quickly and effectively as possible. Establishing a policy that makes participation in board orientation mandatory might go a long way toward strengthening board performance, especially if the policy is supported by an effective process. The policy should stipulate that all new board members have to take part in orientation regardless of their previous board experience.

Results from hundreds of board self-assessments have shown that board orientation is often a weak area of board performance. Unfortunately, it is still not uncommon for board members to learn what they need to know almost entirely on the job. As a result, some spend months as observers rather than as full participants; others make unwise assumptions based on their experiences on other boards — in some cases making old board members resentful of the ways new members participate in deliberations. In either case, both the board and the new members are short-changed.

DISTRIBUTE BOARD HANDBOOKS

Even though some information was hopefully supplied during the recruitment process, once seated on the board, each new member needs to be provided with a more complete set of information. Don't assume that newly elected board members have remembered or kept all the information conveyed during the recruitment process.

Each new board member should receive a board manual, or board handbook, prior to the board orientation session. If the orientation session cannot be scheduled until later, at least make sure that new members receive the board handbook before they attend their first board meeting. The board manual should contain information pertinent to the board and its members and organized as an easy reference. See the Suggested Contents for Board of Directors Handbook on the next page for a listing of materials to include in the handbook.

The board book should also include information about each of the board members, what they bring to the board, and how to contact them. Including a picture along with a biographical summary of each member is a great aid to helping new members integrate into the board. However, it is not advisable to include members' full resumes as this might easily suggest that some board members carry more weight than others. All of this information is designed to help new members understand the context for their board work.

CONDUCT AN ORIENTATION

An effective board orientation requires the involvement of the board chair, the chief executive, the governance committee, and possibly key board and staff members. They may not all be involved at the same time since they have different roles and responsibilities, but it will be important for new board members to understand how each contributes to the work of the board and to the organization.

Board orientation should be facilitated by the board chair since this is the person responsible for guiding the work of the board. The chief executive and senior staff may be best suited to lead an orientation to the work of the organization and its finances. Some organizations invite all current board members to attend all or part of orientation sessions as this can serve as an excellent opportunity for ongoing board education. Long-time board members may be particularly helpful in sharing stories about the past, and even the most experienced board members may find the sessions helpful for keeping them current on new developments or reminding them of things

Suggested Contents for Board of Directors Handbook

A. The board

1. Board member names and contact information
2. Board member bios, using standard format (not formal resumes)
3. Board member terms
4. Statement of board responsibilities
5. Board member responsibilities
6. Committee descriptions

B. Historical references for the organization

1. Brief written history and/or fact sheet
2. Articles of Incorporation
3. IRS determination letter
4. Listing of past board members

C. Bylaws

D. Strategic framework

1. Mission, vision, and values statements
2. Strategic framework or plan
3. Current annual operating plan
4. Programs list

E. Finance

1. Prior year's annual report
2. Prior year's audit report
3. Chart outlining financial growth (sales, membership, programs, etc. — for the past five to 10 years)
4. Current annual budget
5. IRS Form 990
6. Banking resolutions

7. Policies related to investments, reserves, endowments, etc.
8. Risk management policies

F. Policies pertaining to the board

1. Policy on potential conflicts of interest
2. Insurance coverage
3. Legal liability policies
4. Travel/meeting expense reimbursements
5. Accreditation documents if applicable
6. Whistleblower policy
7. Others

G. Staff

1. The chief executive's job description
2. Staff listing (at least senior staff and those with whom the board might interact)
3. Organization/team chart

H. Resource development

1. Case statement
2. Current funder list
3. Sample grant proposal
4. Sponsorship policy

I. Other information

1. Annual calendar
2. Programs list
3. List of common acronyms and terms with explanations
4. Current brochures
5. Web site information

J. Procedures to update board handbook

It would be helpful to have this information available and regularly updated on a secure board page on the organization's Web site.

they may have forgotten. Having at least a few seasoned board members present also serves to build relationships that will help blur the old member/new member divisions.

It is usually best to hold at least part of the orientation at the organization's main office, even if it is only to get a feel for the home office and to meet key staff. A tour of the facility can give new board members a sense of the staff's working environment and the scope of the organization's programs. But if the home office is not an appropriate spot for information sharing and discussion, a quiet, comfortable off-site location should be chosen. Another way to introduce new board members to the organization's services is to pair up a board member with a staff member and shadow this person through a workday.

An orientation session can be tailored to fit varying amounts of time, usually from an hour or two to half a day. The full orientation may be spread out over several sessions to accommodate board member schedules, and avoid information overload. Subjects to be covered include the roles and responsibilities of board members, the organization's mission and programs, its strategic plan, finances, fundraising initiatives, and the structure of the board and staff. The orientation should touch on financial statements and the most recent audit, explain liability and insurance coverage, and reiterate the time commitment involved. Orientation may also include a video presentation on board roles and responsibilities followed by discussion. It is helpful to go over committee job descriptions and goals and to orient new board members on how to be effective committee members.

In addition to formal presentations, leave time for questions and the opportunity for board members to get to know each other. This can be a time for informal sharing of stories from the organization's past to give new members a sense of the events and personalities that helped shape the organization.

It is important to remember that board members, like everyone else, learn at their own speed. In addition to more formal presentations and discussions with the board, accommodate members' different learning styles by offering reading materials, CDs, or videos to be reviewed at their own pace. For help with designing a board orientation, the CD-ROM included with this book features the BoardSource board orientation slide show, *Presenting: Board Orientation*. The PowerPoint® presentation can be easily customized and provides the user with a visual overview of the nonprofit sector, the organization, the board, and the board's roles and responsibilities. This is not intended to be a one-size-fits-all presentation, but rather a basic framework for board orientation. The presentation also includes specific suggestions for customizing the slides and notes with talking points to help guide the facilitator. For more information on the CD-ROM, see the Appendix on page 75.

But there is only so much that can be communicated during a formal orientation. A more informal orientation should take place to help fill in the holes — or cover the things that aren't written down anywhere. The chief executive, board chair, or governance committee chair should make an opportunity sometime after the first board meeting to give new members a sense of the culture of the board and organization and to explain how things really work. The discussion might cover simple things like what people generally wear to board meetings, whether members arrive promptly to meetings, and other insider information — for example, that the board is in the middle of a transition from the founding generation to newer generations. If it wasn't covered in the formal orientation, this could be the time to talk more about the organization's history — the kind not likely to be written down — for instance if the organization went through a turbulent time. It will make new members feel included in "the family" and may make them better understand the background for current practices and relationships.

Orientation should not be a one-time event, but may stretch out as long as a year. During that time, the governance committee might pair up a new board member with a more seasoned member as a mentor who can befriend the new member, make him or her feel welcome, address questions that crop up from time to time, and encourage active participation. A mentor relationship can be particularly helpful in explaining the background of current controversies or the history behind issues that the board needs to address. In order to avoid misunderstandings between mentor and mentee, draft a written description of what each should expect from the relationship.

It is a good idea to schedule a follow-up session several months into the new board member's term to respond to questions now that the member has become more familiar with the organization. The board member might wonder about the history of leadership changes or the organization's relationship to other institutions. This is also a good opportunity to ask new members for feedback on the board's operation. New board members may present wonderful opportunities for rejuvenating the board as they often come asking new questions and bringing fresh ideas that can give the board a fresh perspective on its work. Such follow-up sessions may be brief and informal chats initiated by the board chair, conducted over lunch with the chief executive, or a more formal gathering organized by the governance committee.

The following is an overview of the information that needs to be conveyed to new board members during their orientation with suggestions of various ways in which the information may be communicated. Some issues may be presented in person and other items in writing only or via video or on the Web site. Much of the information can be included in the board manual, but it should also be discussed, or at least referred to, during orientation sessions.

BOARD ORIENTATION CHART

Program

Offer new board members a feel for the work of the organization — what it does, whom it serves, what difference it makes — to get them emotionally and intellectually connected and motivated.

- Tour of facilities

- Observation of/participation in program activities

- Presentation by client, member, or program participant

- Video, slides, film presentation

- Verbal presentations

- Written program descriptions

Finances

Help new board members become informed about where money comes from, how it is spent, and the state of the organization's financial health, including their role in fundraising.

- Presentation by chief executive, chief financial officer, or treasurer

- Background materials (most recent audit, budget, financials), graphically presented, if possible

- Presentation of the fundraising strategy

History

Provide sufficient knowledge about the past so that the present makes sense. Also, help new board members see their own participation as part of the organization's ongoing story.

- Stories told by former board members or long-standing members (in person or on video)

- Pictures

- Written materials covering the basic facts of the organization, e.g., when it was founded and other major historical highlights

Strategic Direction

Present a framework for new members to participate effectively. Clarify the mission, vision, values, and goals that inform the organization's actions.

- Presentation/discussion by the chief executive or board chair

- Copy of strategic plan (or other documents, especially mission statement, if no plan is available)

Organizational Structure

Help new board members understand who does what and lines of accountability.

- Copy of the bylaws, IRS determination letter
- Organizational chart
- Introductions to key staff members

Board Roles

Ensure that new members understand the roles of the board.

- Presentation/discussion, preferably with the whole board involved
- Written materials, CD, video, and/or Web site

Board Member Responsibilities

Ensure that new board members understand their own responsibilities as board members.

- Presentation/discussion
- Signed agreement job description, including conflict-of-interest and ethics statements

Board Operations

Help new board members understand how the board operates so that they may participate effectively.

- Board manual
- Board mentors
- Committee charges and member lists
- Meeting schedule

The Board as a Team

Facilitate new board member integration with the other members.

- List of board members and biographical data
- Time set aside for social interaction

Skills

Instruct new members on how to read a financial statement.

- Written materials including a glossary of common financial terms and a description of the different documents that make up the organization's financials
- Presentation by the treasurer or finance committee

BOARD MEMBER ORIENTATION CHECKLIST

The governance committee should develop a checklist, similar to the following, for use by new board members indicating what they need to take responsibility for learning about during their first three months on the board:

Information	What To Do	When Completed
Program	☐ Tour of facilities ☐ Presentation by chief executive, key staff, video, or other electronic media ☐ Written materials	_____ _____ _____
Finances	☐ Presentation by chief executive, chief financial officer, or treasurer ☐ Review of recent financials ☐ Learn how to read and understand financial statements	_____ _____ _____
History	☐ Read written materials	_____
Strategic Direction	☐ Review of strategic plan	_____
Organizational Structure	☐ Review of bylaws ☐ Review of organizational chart ☐ Introduction to key staff members	_____ _____ _____
Board Roles	☐ Review of written materials ☐ Discussion with board chair or whole board	_____ _____
Board Member Responsibilities	☐ Signed letter of agreement ☐ Signed conflict-of-interest policy	_____ _____
Board Operations	☐ Review of board manual ☐ Meeting with board chair ☐ Accept committee or task force assignment ☐ Attend board meetings	_____ _____ _____ _____

Step 4: Action Steps

- Conduct a new board member orientation as soon as possible after election.

- Provide new board members with a board member handbook prior to the board orientation session.

- Consider assigning board mentors to each of the new members to help answer questions and provide a friendly transition onto the board.

- Take time to communicate information about the culture of the board, such as how members dress for meetings, how they relate to parliamentary procedure, and expected participation in other events and activities.

- Plan a follow-up orientation session later in the year to help answer new members' questions and listen to their feedback about the operations of the board.

Step 5: Involve

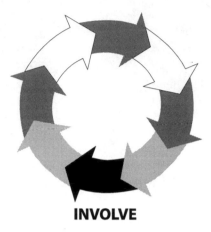

INVOLVE

While people might agree to join in order to affiliate with a mission, they are more apt to participate when they can see the results of their work and the opportunity to have influence.

— Richard P. Chait, William P. Ryan, and Barbara E. Taylor
  Governance as Leadership

Individual commitment to a group effort — that is what makes a team work, a company work, a society work, a civilization work.

— Vince Lombardi
  1913 – 1970 U.S. Football Coach

GET EVERYONE ENGAGED WITH THE WORK OF THE BOARD

Getting new board members actively involved early on can build on the momentum of the orientation and tap into their initial enthusiasm. However, keeping long-standing members continually challenged to do their best is equally important. Board members — both old and new — need to be engaged with important work on the board in order to have a stake in it. And without a stake, board service will be uninspired and pro forma.

Experience tells us that board members want and need to feel a personal connection to the organization and its services, but also that it takes inspiration to keep them involved and engaged. Some of this inspiration comes from realizing that the board makes a difference in helping the organization serve the mission and that they each personally make a difference in the work of the board.

During a recent workshop on board effectiveness, a young woman told the group about her growing ambivalence about her board service. While she was proud to be affiliated with an organization doing wonderful work in the community, she did not think the board had much to do with the organization's accomplishments. "As a matter of fact," she said, "I don't think anything would change if the board did not meet for two or three years." As a result she sometimes decided to let other commitments take precedence over board meeting attendance. "I am thinking about resigning from my board," another added, "because I leave board meetings feeling useless. I feel like I am basically there to fill a slot, which is not what I had in mind when I agreed to serve."

Inspiration for active engagement also comes from connecting one's own hopes and aspirations with the board's activities. Board leaders need to try to link board members with activities that will help them achieve their own goals as well as those of the organization. Such linkage takes place in board meetings, in committee and task force work, and in individual assignments. This means that board chairs and chief executives need to get to know board members in order to make appropriate use of their skills. What was it that made new members say yes to board service? What are they hoping to gain in return for the time and effort they will be expected to expend? Are there time constraints or other factors that may limit their participation?

DEVELOP WAYS OF INVOLVING BOARD MEMBERS

First of all, to keep board members engaged, board meetings need to involve their participation. Meetings should be structured in such a way that board members feel that their time is well spent, and that something has been accomplished by the time they leave — something that will make a difference for the organization. Effective board meetings have

- clearly stated objectives for each meeting

- agendas that focus on strategic issues rather than on "administrivia"

- use of consent agendas for routine decisions and reports rather than the board spending time listening to reports

- time set aside for questions and discussion, for considering implications of information or proposals

- an opportunity for learning something new and relevant to the mission or to organizational effectiveness

- general participation rather than a few people who dominate the discussion

- a chair who keeps the discussion focused and moving forward without stifling thoughtful and creative participation

Keeping board members engaged also means making productive use of committees and task forces so that everyone's time, talent, and interests can be effectively used. Giving board members a specific job to do — whether on a standing committee that meets throughout the year or on a task force with a short-term project — can mean the difference between their feeling connected to a worthwhile endeavor and being a detached spectator. A member of the program evaluation committee might be asked to find out how another board has tackled a similar task. A person with experience in human resource administration might be glad to serve on a short-term task force to review the current human resource policy. Not only will they have the satisfaction of making a difference, they will also get to know a small group of board members better and have the opportunity to gain the respect of their peers.

When making committee assignments, keep the individual in mind. Does the committee offer an opportunity to make a difference based on an individual's expertise or perspective? Does it offer an opportunity for the member to learn something or get more connected to other board members? Does the individual have time to devote to regular meetings, or does the person's schedule suggest assignment to a task force, whose work may be done over a shorter period of time? These days, busy people are particularly enthusiastic about assignments that are specific and time-limited. This allows board members to see the results of their work more easily and become involved in a variety of issues over time.

Board member involvement may take the form of individual initiatives and assignments. Making needed expertise available to the chief executive or other key staff members, or participating in activities of the organization, may boost an individual's sense of commitment. A chief executive looking to hire a new chief financial officer might need help in reviewing candidates and would value the participation of a board member with accounting expertise. A business owner might be helpful in developing funding strategies for a new program. Specific activities, such as selling tickets at a festival, spending a day answering phones, or accompanying a staff person on a visit to a legislator, can bring board members closer to the mission and be educational opportunities. But it is important to remember that when board members accept an assignment outside of their board work, they function as volunteers with no more power or authority than other volunteers and should not impose their authority or intervene in the directives set by the chief executive or other staff.

SOLICIT FEEDBACK AND ENCOURAGE GOOD COMMUNICATION

Boring and routine meetings are likely to evaporate initial board member enthusiasm and sow the seeds of emotional or intellectual withdrawal. One way a board can improve its meetings is to take a couple of minutes at the end to collect meeting evaluations; then at the beginning of the next meeting report those results so that board members are aware of ways in which to do better. Step 7 in this book covers this in more depth.

Whether in board meetings, in committee work, or through their individual assignments, new board members (as well as long-standing board members) should be encouraged to ask questions. In particular, after a few months on the board, new members should be asked for feedback. Do they think the orientation covered everything they needed to know? Do they feel their skills are being used to the best advantage? Do they have ample opportunity to discuss important issues? What have they found most rewarding about their board experience so far? What would they change? Ask for specific examples of how the board currently motivates (or could motivate) its members. Solicit comments about specific activities that they have found useful and why. The governance committee and the board chair should agree on who will be responsible for this orientation follow-up and for taking corrective action, if indicated.

Active involvement requires staying informed about subjects the board needs to address. Effective use of technology can help in this regard.

To make sure that some board members are not placed at a significant disadvantage by their geographic distance or by the travel demands of their jobs, board and committee meetings might sometimes be conducted by teleconference or video conference. Such meetings need to be carefully planned, with informational materials sent out ahead, and with guidelines for how to participate in the meeting. Issues that are likely to engender a high degree of emotional response or controversy may best be reserved for face-to-face meetings.

Keeping board members informed and involved between meetings can also be achieved through the use of e-mail. However, boards are also beginning to realize that guidelines are needed on the effective use of e-mail to avoid information overload and other problems. If board members regularly e-mail their board colleagues everything they come across related to the organization's mission area, people will soon stop reading it and may fail to notice when they really need to read shows up in their inbox . Because it is too easy to forward an item by mistake, issues that need to be treated with confidentiality may not be good candidates for e-mail.

Increasingly, organizations are providing the board with secure pages on their Web site. Information specific to the board is posted to these password-protected pages. They provide members with easy access to materials they need to prepare for board discussions, and they support their committee work and special projects. For more on using technology in the boardroom, see Step 6.

To help board members fully realize the importance of their work, make it clear from the start that they are expected to participate and to follow through on assignments. Hold them accountable for the responsibilities they take on. If assignments don't get done, but no one on the board says anything about it, the responsible person may conclude his or her participation isn't very valuable.

Not only is it important to encourage people to get involved in areas where they can use their expertise, have opportunities for learning, personal growth, and leadership development, it is also important to be sure that the work is well dispersed among board members. If too much power and decision making is concentrated with the board chair or a few select board members, others may lose interest. For this reason, it is essential that the chair assign specific tasks and responsibilities and hold board members accountable.

WORK TO DEVELOP THE BOARD AS AN INCLUSIVE TEAM

Building an effective board means building and developing a team composed of the diversity of perspectives, expertise, and other resources needed to accomplish the mission. However, it is not enough to *recruit* a diverse board. The board must become a cohesive unit that makes use of what every board member can offer. Such boards are well positioned to enable creative thinking, innovation, and problem solving and to provide leadership in meeting organizational challenges and identifying new opportunities. The more diverse the board, the more important it is to nurture understanding by creating opportunities for social and interpersonal interaction.

There are two caveats to creating an inclusive board: Avoid tokenism and manage differences of opinion.

Creating a sense of ownership is difficult if board members feel they were recruited purely to represent a part of the constituency. Board members and senior staff must learn to make use of all of the abilities and expertise present among members of the board, not be side-tracked by the visible signs of difference represented by ethnic and generational identities.

To avoid tokenism, treat each board member equally. Involve new members right away and assign them tasks that are independent of their cultural or ethnic background. For example, refrain from turning to the sole Asian board member only when questions come up that relate directly to the Asian community. He or she should be asked to address general questions posed to the board as well as questions related to his or her special expertise — which may or may not have anything in particular to do with the Asian community.

A natural byproduct of inclusiveness may be wider disagreement among members, which is not necessarily easy to deal with. In her article "Inclusion: Encouraging Participatory Governance" in *The New England Nonprofit Quarterly*, Zora Radosevich suggested that inclusiveness means not only bringing in new and different people, but supporting people who say new things and being willing to be uncomfortable while working toward an understanding. With the board chair as moderator, the board needs to cultivate an atmosphere of acceptance by encouraging wide-ranging opinions and molding them into creative solutions. By exploring a variety of perspectives and options, the board is more likely to make effective decisions. For example, the board of an organization dealing with workforce development issues may need to wrestle with the differences between the perspectives of employers and union members. Actions that are taken based solely on the perspectives of one of these groups are likely to be unrealistic and ineffective. Each group's opinions may vary widely, and there may not be consensus. But providing an opportunity to explore each other's views and having a shared commitment to the mission will likely result in a stronger team by the time a solution is reached. Ultimately what counts is that each board member respects the process and supports the position taken by the board because all the different voices were heard.

MAKE USE OF RETREATS

To support the development of the team, the board needs to create opportunities for members to interact more informally than is available during regular board meetings. Members need time to get to know each other by sharing stories and comparing experiences. They need to discover the things they have in common and to explore some of the differences between them. Occasional retreats, if they are scheduled to include as many board members as possible, can serve as powerful team-building events. Whether the focus is on particular topics such as strategic planning, leadership training, board assessments, or a more thorough exploration of important issues, they give board members the chance to gain a better understanding of the board's work and of each other — in other words, to become a more effective team.

Whatever the purpose of the retreat, it requires careful planning. Will it be out-of-town and include overnight accommodations? If so, are there transportation issues for some board members? Are there child care or other dependent care considerations to keep in mind? Are spouses, partners, or children invited? Taking the board overnight to a resort where board members are expected to spend the afternoon playing golf may not be useful for those members who don't play golf, especially if no alternative activities were planned. Even if the retreat is built around a specific set of board issues, make sure there is plenty of time for interaction and for shared social activities. An outside facilitator can help make it possible for everyone, including the chair and the chief executive, to be active participants rather than managers of the board's work.

CLARIFY RESPONSIBILITIES FOR INVOLVING BOARD MEMBERS

Chief responsibility for getting and keeping board members actively and appropriately involved rests with the board chair, but also with the chief executive and committee chairs. By getting to know each member of the board and establishing an open line of communication, the chair is essential to their effective inclusion and engagement. Smart chairs will assign board members to committees according to interest, skill, and available time, and will check in with new board members after a few months to find out if they need additional information and invite their feedback on board operations.

The chief executive often plays an important role in engaging board members by providing necessary information as well as suggesting specific ways in which a member's expertise and interests might be of particular service to the organization. For example, the board chair of a youth service organization may ask a board member who lives in the neighborhood of its youth center to serve as the organization's eyes and ears and to keep the staff informed of issues that could lead to conflict. This type of involvement often leads to a board member's greater sense of contribution and commitment.

Since much of the board's work is often conducted outside of board meetings by committees and task forces, the chairs of these groups are instrumental in helping board members to become active participants. By calling, organizing, and facilitating productive meetings where everyone is heard and work gets done, they help provide a sense of accomplishment and belonging. Asking individual members to take on specific tasks on behalf of the committee can provide a welcome challenge. When someone does not show up for meetings or follow through with assignments, good chairs will check in with the person to find out if there is a problem. A telephone call after a meeting saying, "We missed you last night. I hope everything is all right" will not only remind the member that there is work to be done, but also that his or her absence was noticed. It might also provide an opportunity for the member to bring up problems that need to be addressed or to clear up misunderstandings.

Particularly with larger boards, the role of committees and small groups plays an important part of providing board members, both old and new, with opportunities to get to know each other and to be part of a team. However, no matter what the size of the board, all leaders share in the responsibility of actively involving and mobilizing their members in the work of the board.

STEP 5: ACTION STEPS

- Provide opportunities for active participation through interactive board meetings.

- Focus the board on strategically important issues.

- Involve board members on committees and task forces.

- Make information easily available to the board.

- Create opportunities for social interaction, sharing of experience, and exploration of ideas.

INVOLVING BOARD MEMBERS

1. Conduct board meetings that focus on strategic issues and get important things done.

2. Encourage all board members to ask questions and actively participate in board discussions.

3. Be honest in expressing your opinions.

4. Build relationships that foster trust and promote accountability.

5. Engage new members in meaningful activities based on their skills, talents, and interests.

6. Follow sound board development practices to create a positive working climate for all board members.

7. Develop effective communication processes for quick information dissemination and responses.

BARRIERS TO KEEPING BOARD MEMBERS INVOLVED

- The board is too large. Some board members do not feel needed.

- The board is too small. Board members feel overwhelmed or suffer from insufficient stimulation or limited perspectives.

- The executive committee is too active. If it meets too often, the rest of the board may feel like a rubber stamp or disengaged.

- Members received insufficient or ineffective orientation.

- Agendas are weak. They lack substance, are too long or too routine. Board members fail to see the relevance of board meeting topics to organizational performance.

- Members do not feel well used or important. They will decide that they have better things to do.

- There is little or no opportunity for discussion. Board members feel bored or frustrated.

- A few board members are allowed to monopolize discussion, to take up disproportional amounts of airtime, and carry disproportional weight in decisions.

- The board lacks social glue. Board members have little in common except board service and do not have opportunities to get to know each other.

- Status differences get in the way of team development.

- Board members lack passion for the mission.

- Board participation has become routine after many years of service.

Step 6: Educate

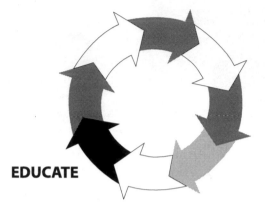

EDUCATE

We get so tied up in today's needs that we don't reserve a realistic part of our resources for developing the talent and dedication necessary to carry out and expand the organization's efforts tomorrow.

—Brian O'Connell
   The Board Member's Book

Real learning gets to the heart of what it means to be human. Through learning we re-create ourselves. Through learning we become able to do something we never were able to do.

—Peter Senge
   The Fifth Discipline

CREATE REGULAR OPPORTUNITIES FOR BOARD EDUCATION

To survive and thrive in a rapidly changing and ever more complex society, education and continued learning are keys to making good decisions, yet this step is often overlooked by boards. While most board members were asked to join the board because of their knowledge and success, they often come to the board lacking an understanding of the intricacies of the nonprofit organization they are asked to serve. For instance, board members of a ballet company — even the most avid fans — may have no idea how a ballet company is run and may be embarrassed to ask. Consumer board members of a community health center may know a lot about the services provided by the center but may lack an understanding of national health care policy. Board members of a national membership association may be aware of what the membership wants, but have little sense of the financial implications involved in various service options. In some cases, board members may be unaware of issues facing the nonprofit sector in general or of the need for strategic leadership.

As pointed out in the BoardSource publication, *The Source: Twelve Principles of Governance That Power Exceptional Boards*, continuous learning is a key characteristic of boards that stand out from the crowd. Such boards understand the need for expanding and deepening their members' knowledge about factors that will have an impact on the organization's success in the long run. They build educational activities into board meetings, schedule retreats for exploration of complicated issues, and encourage their members to attend outside workshops and seminars. In such ways the board stays well informed and supported in its planning and decision-making responsibilities. In such ways organizational leaders learn and grow, and in turn their organizations learn and grow.

Topics for board education might range from internal issues such as fundraising, strategic planning, liability issues, or how to read a financial statement to external issues such as demographic trends, mission-related challenges, and emerging competition. Instead of looking at financial statements only to discover whether income and expenses are in balance, forward-looking boards learn to look for information that gives clues about the organization's long-term financial health. Instead of looking at changes in the community's population from the perspective of who will need the organization's services, learning-oriented boards seek to understand how such changes will have an impact on economic and political structures as well as on the community's culture. Hospital boards need to learn not only about new developments in health care but also about factors that influence the supply of physicians, nurses, and other health care personnel and about health care financing.

STRENGTHEN FROM WITHIN

In addition to learning about big societal issues and developments, each board also needs to keep learning about how it can strengthen its own performance. This, like the board building cycle, is a never-ending process. No board can afford to believe that it has arrived at perfection, that it has no more to learn about being a great board. Jim Collins says that "good is the enemy of great" and implies that greatness is as much a process as a destination. When a group feels that it has arrived and can begin to coast, circumstances can change and the sands can start to shift underneath the group.

Some topics can be scheduled for discussion as part of regular board agendas throughout the year; others may emerge suddenly because of decisions that need to be made. For example, board consultant Bruce Lesley suggests that if a board realizes that it needs to develop or revise its conflict-of-interest policy, a short educational piece on the board's legal duties might be very effective because of its immediate relevance. If a local hospice is approached by a hospice in a neighboring community about merging the two organizations, the board needs to learn quickly about issues related to mergers and about the other organization.

To keep a board in a learning mode, members should be encouraged to suggest topics that would help them and the board do a better job. To keep suggestions coming, ask for ideas during meeting evaluations, board self-assessments, and exit interviews conducted when board members step down. In their book *Improving the Performance of Governing Boards*, Richard P. Chait, Thomas P. Holland, and Barbara E. Taylor cite an independent school that used a "pop quiz" to prompt suggestions. The quiz contained 30 basic questions about the school, such as gender balance and curriculum requirements. The board members were not required to share their scores because the object of the quiz was to show them where there were important gaps in their knowledge and to encourage them to request programs and activities to fill those gaps.

Some form of education should be on the agenda of nearly every board meeting, whether a presentation by an outside consultant or a briefing by a staff member on developments in the organization's mission area. A museum board might enjoy a presentation about the way another museum increased attendance. Someone from an affiliate across the country might talk about industry trends. A funder might make a presentation about the need to measure and document outcomes or about factors used to evaluate grant proposals. A government official could provide an update on pending legislation on an issue such as tax deduction for charitable contributions. Or an educational researcher might present new findings related to gender issues in elementary education.

In another approach, board members might be assigned as individuals or as groups to explore certain subjects and then report their findings to the full board. For example, an adult literacy board preparing for a strategic planning retreat might assign a group of board members to dig up statistics on changing demographics and employment issues. The board of a local YMCA might assign several of its members to gather and present information about financing options for a major renovation of the facilities.

Whatever approach is chosen for particular topics, set aside time for discussion. Rather than just asking for questions and comments after a presentation, it is usually more effective to ask the board to discuss the possible implications of the information presented, to consider how the topic relates to the strategic plan, or to brainstorm questions that need further exploration.

Some educational activities might need to be conducted in executive session behind closed doors if there is a need for off-the-record information sharing or an exploration of emerging issues or topics of a sensitive nature, such as a possible merger or options that may have legal implications. These sessions will usually include the chief executive. However, the board's meeting with the auditor to review the annual audit and to learn how to make more effective use of financial statements ought to take place in executive session without the chief executive present. Meeting in private can allow board members to talk more candidly and to raise questions. However, organizations in states with "sunshine laws" will need to ensure that such sessions do not violate the open meetings requirements.

EXPERIENCE SOME HANDS-ON EDUCATION

Field trips are an excellent way to help the board understand the organization's programs and the needs they address. Having board members see programs and services in action, meet with individuals benefiting from these programs, or travel to the organization's different sites has a way of making the issues and needs come alive. Participating as a group in one of the organization's programs will serve the same purpose. When board members of a public television station staff the phone bank for an evening during pledge week, or board members of a theater company serve as ushers on a Saturday evening, or board members of a homeless shelter put on a holiday party for clients, they not only learn but gain personal satisfaction from making a tangible contribution.

Wise organizations put money in the budget for board development activities. For example, the Association of Fund Raising Professionals, based in Arlington, Virginia, holds frequent workshops across the country to help people learn fundraising techniques and trends. Resources for board education related to the craft of organizational governance include BoardSource, local management support organizations, some colleges and universities, and individual consultants. Such resources can be brought directly to an individual board, but board members can also be encouraged to attend more public events. National and regional associations frequently include workshops related to governance in their conferences. In collaboration with local partner organizations, BoardSource sometimes holds workshops in different parts of the country on a variety of subjects, providing board member training and opportunities for board members from different organizations to meet and share ideas. The BoardSource annual Board Leadership Forum brings together board leaders from around the country to learn about latest developments in nonprofit governance and to learn about the experience of other boards.

MAKE THE BEST USE OF TECHNOLOGY

More and more boards are keeping connected electronically. Many are putting money in the budget for laptops, modems, and printers for board members who do not already have access to such equipment. Some boards may only consider nominating individuals who can communicate electronically. Computers are used for information sharing on issues, updates, and routine decisions, among other things.

New technologies can free the board to do what authors Chait, Holland, and Taylor refer to as the "new work of the board" — discovering the issues that really matter, establishing institutional priorities, and having meetings driven by goals rather than established procedures. The following are examples of information technologies that can help keep the board connected and can contribute to the education of the board:

- **Teleconferencing** can bring together groups of board members for discussions between meetings, but it is not always a good idea to use this medium for conducting larger meetings.

- **Distance-learning programs** via the Internet or satellite technologies can be used for board orientations and leadership training.

- **E-mail**, particularly for boards that are spread out across a state, the country, or throughout the world, may be the most cost-effective way of staying in touch between meetings. By now, even for the technologically challenged, e-mail is no longer unthinkable. It can greatly speed up a board's ability to communicate and provide quick feedback on issues. However, important or lengthy board discussions should not be relegated to e-mail communication, but rather reserved for face-to-face meetings. The board should also establish a policy on what kinds of topics and decisions the board should address online.

- **Listservs** and chat technology are online vehicles for engaging like-minded people in issue-oriented conversations and can benefit an organization's membership as well as its board. While this technology can be slower in achieving responses, it can also allow for better information distribution between board meetings.

- **Web sites** can engage board members and help keep them apprised of an organization's programmatic accomplishments. In addition, some organizations designate special password-protected areas of their Web sites for specific communication to board members, making information available to the board when it is needed. This site may include links and information about the community or industry, new developments or regulations affecting the nonprofit sector, or internal documents for the board's review.

New technologies can provide opportunities for learning and for the exchange of ideas and information, but they can never replace the human factor that the board experiences in face-to-face interactions. This is particularly true when a board consists of a wide diversity of perspectives and backgrounds where members may not express themselves in the same way, share the same assumptions, or define words in the same way. What one person might perceive as a rude brush-off, another might consider being admirably succinct.

STEP 6: ACTION STEPS

- Build in opportunities for the board to expand its knowledge, awareness, and understanding.

- Educate board members on external issues that might affect the organization and the mission as well as on specific board functions.

- Make information readily available to board members through e-mail or on a password-protected Web site.

- Organize activities that get board members involved and teach them things outside of the regular boardroom context.

Step 7: Evaluate

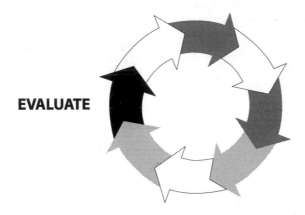

EVALUATE

Exceptional boards embrace the qualities of a continuous learning organization, evaluating their own performance and assessing the value they add to the organization.

— *The Source: Twelve Principles of Governance That Power Exceptional Boards*

ASSESS THE BOARD'S PERFORMANCE

There is no such thing as a board that has "arrived" that cannot or should not continue to grow. This is particularly true now when every organization exists in an environment of almost constant change and challenge. To serve as effective leadership bodies, boards cannot afford complacency. Wise boards take time for regular check-ups to discover ways to strengthen their performance. Using regular board meeting evaluations, formal self-assessments, and feedback from outside consultants, these boards keep discovering ways in which to increase their value to the organization and to their own members.

EVALUATE BOARD MEETINGS

Since conducting effective board meetings is critical to effective board performance, every board ought to institute a practice of regular board meeting evaluations. It takes just a few minutes at the end of the meeting to fill out feedback forms or for a quick round of member comments about what worked well and what might need improvement. Generally, the feedback should relate to whether the meeting dealt with issues of substance and strategic importance, whether it was run efficiently and whether it used board members' time wisely. Was the agenda well organized? Did members receive background materials in advance? Did the meeting begin and end on time? Was everyone's voice heard, or did a few members dominate the discussion? Were issues discussed and debated, or did the board mostly listen to reports from staff and/or committees? Was something achieved?

To get quick feedback at the end of a meeting the chair might ask everyone to complete these two phrases: "The thing I most liked about this meeting was ......" and "One thing that could have improved this meeting was ......" This exercise asks for board members to write down their responses on index cards and then either to read their responses aloud or simply hand them in at the end. It is sometimes very useful to hear everyone's immediate feedback to identify whether there is general consensus or whether the board is divided on what is or is not effective.

To make effective use of meeting evaluations, a board could start out by determining what would constitute a very good board meeting. A list of such characteristics can then easily be turned into a simple board meeting evaluation form. After collecting the completed forms at the end of a meeting, the chair compiles the responses, and if necessary, takes corrective action in planning the next meeting. The chair also provides a summary of the feedback before the next meeting so that everyone is reminded of the board's commitment to make more effective and efficient use of the time together. A sample board meeting evaluation is found on page 59.

Developing and implementing a set of board meeting agreements also supports the chair in conducting effective meetings. For example, the agreement may state that a few people are not allowed to dominate a discussion. The chair can then enforce this with a comment such as, "We've heard Robert's and Keith's opinions, but let's find out what the rest of the board thinks. I am going to go around the table and ask each of you to briefly state how you see this issue." By holding the board to its own set of standards, it can usually see significant improvements in meeting culture and in the level of satisfaction among board members.

CONDUCT A BOARD ASSESSMENT

A more thorough assessment of the board's performance in all areas of its responsibilities should take place every two to three years . It should review how well the board has carried out its responsibilities and therefore how well it has served the organization and, equally important, how it could do better. The assessment should examine the composition of the board, how well the board identifies and recruits new members, whether it has a good relationship with its constituents and the chief executive, whether the committee structure works, and whether the meetings are well run. In addition, some important questions the board should answer include the following:

- To what extent are board members clear about the roles and responsibilities of the board?

- Are board members familiar with and in support of the current mission statement? Is the current mission statement appropriate for the organization's role in the next two to four years?

- Has the board been engaged in establishing the organization's strategic direction? Does the board have a strategic vision of how the organization should be evolving over the next three to five years?

- Is the board knowledgeable about the organization's programs? Is there an effective process for tracking program performance?

- Does the board understand the financial resource strategy for the organization? If the organization engages in fundraising, do all board members make a financial contribution to the organization or participate in fundraising activities and solicitations?

- Does the board ensure that the budget reflects the organization's priorities established in the strategic or annual plan? Are there appropriate financial controls set in place? Has the board established appropriate investment policies? Risk management policies?

- Does the board regularly assess the chief executive's performance? Has the chief executive's compensation been determined in an objective and adequate manner? Are there clear divisions between board and staff roles?

Particular times when board assessments can be especially critical are

- in the early stages of the organization's life, especially when the organization has hired staff after having been largely volunteer-run;

- when there is some confusion about which responsibilities belong to the board and which to the staff;

- during changes in leadership (either on the board or in the chief executive position); and

- in connection with strategic planning.

To start the board thinking about assessing its performance it is sometimes a good idea to begin with a brief mini-assessment, such as the one found on page 60. The mini-assessment provides a quick look at whether board members perceive the board's performance in the same way and whether they think the board needs to strengthen its performance in any particular areas. However, the short form does not adequately spell out what the board does to fulfill its responsibilities in each area and may present the board with a glossy picture of its performance. Responses should be tallied and the results discussed with the board. Ideally, a mini-assessment will serve as a catalyst to a full scale self-assessment.

Board assessments are not meant to be report cards. They are designed to serve a developmental purpose, to assist the board in identifying ways to strengthen its performance. For that reason, the key component of the assessment is the board's *self*-assessment. The initiative for a board self-assessment may come from the governance committee, the chief executive, the chair, or any member of the board who has heard how such a process can help boards improve. Once the board agrees to undertake the assessment, it needs to decide what kind of instrument to use for gathering feedback from its members and identify who will be responsible for collecting and compiling responses. All members of the board are then asked to complete the assessment survey and should be encouraged to be completely forthcoming in their opinions. Most boards prefer to keep responses anonymous in order to encourage candid responses. Board members' responses are then compiled in a report that should give a fairly accurate impression of how the board views its performance. The report will indicate areas of consensus and areas where board members differ about how well the board is doing in exercising its responsibilities. The assessment should culminate in an extended board session or a retreat where the board has time to discuss and identify steps toward increased effectiveness.

Many boards invite an outside governance consultant to facilitate the assessment process. This helps provide a wider perspective on the board's performance and brings fresh ideas to the board's efforts to strengthen its operations. The consultant can collect and summarize board member feedback, seek the chief executive's perspective on how well the board is doing in the various areas of responsibilities, and facilitate the board's discussion of its assessment report. A consultant knowledgeable about nonprofit governance can add valuable insights and assist in developing strategies for improvement.

OUTCOMES OF THE ASSESSMENT PROCESS

Board assessments can serve a number of functions: They can measure the board's progress, identify areas that need improving, and establish goals for the future. They can also remind members of their responsibilities as board members and help re-shape the board's operations. Discussion of the results can also help the board to build trust and facilitate communication among its members and the chief executive. Board assessments represent time and effort well spent and, in the long run, can save money by making better use of limited resources and helping to ensure the organization's health and viability in a changing world. BoardSource publishes several board self-assessment instruments, at least one of which is presented as an online survey (see Suggested Resources on page 76).

Common outcomes of board assessments include

- strategic planning initiatives

- improvements in monitoring program effectiveness

- enhanced board meetings and a more effective use of committees

- improvements in the process for reviewing the chief executive's performance

- strategies for more intentional board recruitment

- establishment of a governance committee and of a more thoughtful nomination process

MEASURE INDIVIDUAL BOARD MEMBER PERFORMANCE

In addition to evaluating the performance of the board as a whole, there is also the question of individual board member performance. Individual assessments are particularly useful when a board member's term is about to end and he or she is being considered for re-election. As the governance committee prepares for an upcoming board election, it is wise to ask each incumbent who is eligible for another term to complete a self-evaluation. This self-evaluation may be based on the board member letter of agreement that members signed at the beginning of their term if any, the board member job description, or the individual board member section of the board self-assessment instrument. The self-evaluation and a subsequent conversation with the board chair serve several purposes: to assist incumbents in considering whether they ought to stand for re-election, to remind them of their responsibilities if they were to be elected for an additional term, and to help the governance committee determine whether to nominate a member for an additional term.

Because of the current emphasis on accountability and the increased awareness of boards operating as teams, some boards now engage in peer evaluations, particularly in connection with renomination of current members. Peer evaluation forms are usually brief and commonly ask about attendance, preparation, follow-through on assignments, and quality of participation in board discussions and interaction with other board members and staff. Most commonly collected and summarized by the chair, the results are shared with each individual evaluated and also with the governance committee in preparation for possible renomination. Individuals who are evaluated by their peers gain valuable insights into how they are perceived by others and have the option of modifying their behavior accordingly. However, because board members serve on a voluntary basis, many may feel uncomfortable or resentful of being held up for judgment by their peers. For this reason, the practice of peer evaluation is still fairly uncommon.

STEP 7: ACTION STEPS

- To help promote the board's continuous growth and improvement, take time to reflect on the board's performance and that of individual members.

- Establish criteria for what the board considers to be an effective meeting and then regularly evaluate meetings based on these criteria.

- Conduct a full-scale board assessment every two to three years. Invite an outside facilitator to assist the board in determining how to use assessment results to strengthen its performance.

- Consider administering self-assessments to board members seeking re-election.

BOARD MEETING EVALUATION FORM

To assist the board in making effective and efficient use of board meeting time, please take a couple of minutes to fill in this questionnaire and leave it on the table before you depart.

		OK	Needs Improvement	Suggestions for Improvement
1.	The agenda focused on issues of long-term importance, was supported by the necessary documents.			
2.	The meeting materials were circulated in sufficient time prior to the meeting.			
3.	All board members were prepared to discuss materials sent in advance.			
4.	Reports were clear and contained needed information.			
5.	We avoided getting into administrative/management details.			
6.	A diversity of opinions were expressed and issues were dealt with in a respectful manner.			
7.	The chair guided the meeting effectively.			
8.	Members participated responsibly.			
9.	Next steps were identified and responsibility assigned.			
10.	A substantial majority of board members were present.			
11.	The meeting began and ended on time.			
12.	The meeting room was conducive to work.			
13.	I am glad I came. It was a worthwhile use of my time.			

MINI BOARD SELF-ASSESSMENT SURVEY

Review the list of basic board responsibilities. Indicate whether, in your opinion, the board currently does a good job in an area or whether the board needs to improve its performance.

	DOES WELL	NEEDS WORK	NOT SURE
Organization's Mission			
Do we use it as a guide for decisions?	☐	☐	☐
Does it need to be revised?	☐	☐	☐
Strategic Planning			
Do we have a clear sense of direction? Have we approved major goals?	☐	☐	☐
Have we established measurements for monitoring progress?	☐	☐	☐
Program Evaluation			
Do we have criteria for determining program effectiveness?	☐	☐	☐
Financial Resources			
Do we understand the organization's income strategy?	☐	☐	☐
Do all board members participate actively in fundraising efforts?	☐	☐	☐
Fiscal Oversight and Risk Management			
Does the budget reflect our strategic priorities?	☐	☐	☐
Do we have a firm understanding of the organization's financial health?	☐	☐	☐
Relationship with the Chief Executive			
Is there a climate of mutual trust and respect between the board and the chief executive?	☐	☐	☐
Does the executive receive a fair and comprehensive annual performance review?	☐	☐	☐
Board-Staff Relationship			
Do all board members refrain from attempting to direct members of the staff?	☐	☐	☐
Do board and staff treat each other with respect?	☐	☐	☐
Public Relations and Advocacy			
Are all board members actively promoting the organization in the community?	☐	☐	☐
Do we understand the organization's public relations strategy?	☐	☐	☐
Board Selection and Orientation			
Does the board have the necessary diversity of perspectives and other resources needed?	☐	☐	☐
Do new board members get an effective orientation?	☐	☐	☐
Board Organization			
Do board meetings make effective use of the time and talents of board members?	☐	☐	☐
Do our committees contribute to the effective functioning of the board?	☐	☐	☐

INDIVIDUAL BOARD MEMBER SELF-EVALUATION FORM

Use the following questions for individual board member evaluation. Board members answering yes to these questions are likely to be fulfilling their responsibilities as board members.

		Yes	No	Not Sure
1.	Do I understand and support the mission of the organization?			
2.	Am I sufficiently knowledgeable about the organization's programs and services?			
3.	Do I follow trends and important developments related to this organization?			
4.	Do I assist with fundraising and/or give a significant annual gift to the organization?			
5.	Do I stay informed about the organization's financial health?			
6.	Do I have a good working relationship with the chief executive?			
7.	Do I recommend individuals for service to this board?			
8.	Do I prepare for and participate in board meetings and committee meetings?			
9.	Do I act as a good-will ambassador for the organization?			
10.	Do I find serving on the board to be a satisfying and rewarding experience?			
11.	Do I attend at least 75% of board meetings during the year?			

Step 8: Rotate

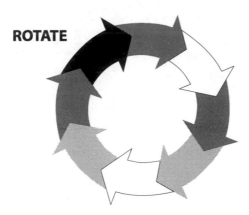

ROTATE

*If we get the right people on the bus, the right people in the right seats,
and the wrong people off the bus, then we'll figure out how to take it
someplace great.*

—Jim Collins
   Good to Great and the Social Sectors

KEEP THE BOARD FRESH

In the early stages, board membership can be exhilarating and challenging. However,
over time, if the board remains largely unchanged, it can grow stagnant. But this
doesn't have to happen. There are many ways to keep a board fresh and interesting,
as was discussed in Steps 5 and 6. Some involve shifting board members' roles within
the board, others involve bringing in new members to introduce novel ideas and
challenge old assumptions.

To keep board members from burning out during their tenure on the board, allow
ample opportunity for change. For example, offer them the chance to serve on
different committees, or temporarily suspend their participation on a standing
committee to serve on an ad hoc committee or task force. Giving board members the
chance to chair committees or assume other leadership positions not only helps to
hone their skills and keep them active, but contributes to leadership development
and facilitates succession planning.

An important responsibility of the board chair is to nurture emerging leaders so that
there are viable candidates in line for succession when the time comes. Some organizations use the position of chair-elect to ensure an orderly and regular change in the
chair position. Others use the vice presidency as a similar way of preparing the next

chair. Still other boards prefer to leave the field open until electing the next chair. In the latter case, it is important to appoint a number of board members to positions of responsibility so their colleagues have a way of anticipating how well they would do as a board chair.

Additionally, consider assigning board members to represent the organization on committees or advisory councils outside of the organization. They might also be asked to represent the organization at functions such as community festivals and exhibits or make radio or TV appearances related to specific issues. These external assignments add diversity to board tasks and recognize a member's board service. To support board members with these outside assignments and to give them added confidence, provide them with informational materials, coaching, or role-playing exercises as needed.

MAKE REGULAR ROOM FOR NEW PEOPLE

Over the long term, boards ought to ensure fresh perspectives by the regular infusion of new people. This can be done as a matter of board practice, board policy, or bylaws requirements. Of course, putting new people on the board generally implies that there is an opening. For many boards, openings may happen infrequently and only when someone resigns or chooses not to serve an additional term. The message of this book is that boards need to be more intentional about their composition. Without the structure of setting term limits, it is easy to fall into the habit of keeping a long-time member on the board, even if that person is not able to provide what the board needs.

Almost all organization bylaws stipulate that board members are elected for a specific number of years, but some do not limit the number of times a member may be re-elected. Where this is the case, the board must take extra care that re-elections not become automatic. Board members should be re-elected only if they add sufficient value to the board through their performance and through their possession of attributes needed by the board. Even though a board member knows the organization inside out, is a significant contributor, and is faithful in attending meetings, if the board now needs someone with different skills or perspectives, it may be time for a change and for exploring other ways in which the person can continue to support the organization and its mission.

ADOPT TERM LIMITS

According to the 2004 BoardSource national survey, about two thirds of responding organizations reported using formal term limits. Terms of three years are common, and two consecutive terms of continuous service are often stated as the limit of service. In most cases, board members who reach their term limit can be elected again after at least one year off the board. However, this option should be exercised with care so as not to defeat the purpose of term limits. Re-election should be based on the needs of the board, which may change over time, and a year off the board should not be treated simply as a sabbatical.

There are many reasons to use term limits. They force the board to continually consider what characteristics are needed on the board at a particular time and prevent the board from settling for what it already has, whether or not those characteristics are really needed. They help to continually refresh the board and maintain a balance between continuity and turnover. Term limits can ease the transition from a homogeneous board to a more diverse and inclusive one and thus, in some cases, keep the board in closer touch with its constituents and with the community in which the organization operates. Term limits also provide a painless way to rotate ineffective, inactive, or troublesome members off the board, relieving the governance committee or board chair of the awkward duty of telling them it is time to go.

Though quite common, term limits can be controversial because they pit continuity of board member service, institutional memory, and expertise against the need for new blood and different perspectives. For some organizations, term limits can cause the board to lose valuable board members with hard-to-replace expertise or other helpful resources. This is particularly true of complicated institutions such as hospitals, nursing homes, and credit unions whose board members must acquire a lot of technical expertise during their tenure. It is also true of large organizations with multiple subsidiaries or far-flung operations, such as chapters or affiliates, with which board members need to become familiar. As board members leave, they often take with them a lot of institutional memory. Each board must guard against the loss of such resources by intentionally ensuring that others are developing the skills and knowledge that will enable them to take on the roles vacated by departing board members.

Many organizations have found a way to use term limits both to enforce turnover and to maintain continuity on the board by increasing the number of terms a member can serve to three or four terms. This measure is not intended to ensure every board member the right to serve out a maximum number of terms, rather to help the board retain members who have served in exemplary ways or who bring particular expertise or other resources that are difficult to replicate. The board may want to adopt a formal policy to help board members better understand term limits; for example the policy may state that two- or three three-year terms are the rule, but under unusual circumstances, the governance committee is permitted to nominate someone for an additional term, up to the maximum allowed.

In order to make sure that the whole board does not age in place, some organizations impose an upper-age limit — such as not allowing renominations after the age of 70. That can be controversial and may reflect more on the board's unwillingness to tell a long-time member that he or she will not be renominated than on the capacities of seventy-year-olds, many of whom have a lot to offer, both in terms of wisdom and expertise as well as time for active involvement.

Whether or not an organization operates with term limits, staggering the terms of board members ensures that all existing members will not retire from the board in any given year. How long the terms should be and how many terms are permissible — and, for that matter, whether to use term limits at all — is an issue each board must decide for itself. If term limits are defined in an organization's bylaws, making a change in the length or number of terms permitted will require making a change to the bylaws. On the other hand, boards that have instituted term limits through board policy, rather than bylaws, will have an easier time making adjustments to their current practice. It should be emphasized, however, that whether term limits are stated in the bylaws or by board policy, the board is obligated to follow the practice specified until it is formally changed.

STEP DOWN AND SAY GOOD-BYE

Asking someone to leave is often difficult. A board may be tempted to simply expand its size, particularly when it identifies the need to bring in new expertise or perspectives. But expanding a board that is already at its optimum size is risky. It sets a bad precedent and is likely to lead to a board whose size has become unwieldy, along other problems in the future.

Asking an ineffective or difficult board member to step down from the board is not an easy task. The board chair, not the chief executive, should assume leadership in dealing with such board members. In some cases, a member of the governance committee may want to initiate the conversation. Sometimes board members are aware of their inadequate performance but don't quite know how to handle the idea of resigning. They may feel that resigning implies that they don't care, but they may actually feel relieved when the chair suggests that resigning would be the honorable and generous thing to do. At other times, a friendly conversation can clear up any misunderstandings or false assumptions that may have arisen. See "Removing a Difficult Board Member" on the following page for more information.

Saying good-bye to the board does not have to mean saying good-bye to the organization, or for that matter even entirely to the board. As members leave the board, exit interviews may identify ways in which they could remain connected to the organization. Whether or not an organization imposes term limits, there are several ways to ease someone out of a spot on the board without forever losing their support and influence. One way is to invite them to join a committee, an ad hoc task force, a special President's Council, or to ask them to raise money or volunteer in another capacity.

Bestowing former board members with an "emeritus" or "honorary" status for their outstanding work or financial contributions can be a wonderful way to thank them and to continue to benefit from their expertise, institutional memory, and generosity. As such, they may remain involved with the board, be invited to board meetings, and have a voice — but no vote. But this type of recognition should be done sparingly. In order to have effective discussions, the board needs to guard against having too many people around the table. It is also hard to chart new courses when the leaders of the past are still at the table. If the emeritus position is created, it is wise to limit a person's tenure to no more than a couple of years. This will give the board the continued benefit of the person's wisdom, but also make it clear that it is a transitional status.

While it doesn't happen often, there are times when the whole board needs to be encouraged or even forced to resign. This may be the case when lapses in oversight failed to uncover major ethical and legal problems. In order for the organization to rebuild the public's trust, funding agencies or public oversight bodies might require the whole board to resign. In other situations, the board might feel that it has run out of steam or that it took the organization as far as it could but was not prepared or equipped to take the organization to the next level. Seemingly unsolvable board conflicts concerning the organization's future may also result in an agreement for the whole board to step down. In one such situation there was a significant difference of opinion between the founding chief executive and the board concerning the long-term future of the organization. The board decided to step down and, before resigning, elected a few new board members that were nominated by the founder. This left a skeleton board in place that was able to move forward on the rebuilding phase. These situations are never easy, but the organization's mission and future effectiveness is more important than a board member's pride or the fear of what might happen once he or she lets go.

Occasionally, when a well-liked chief executive steps down, the board will offer him or her board membership as a special lifetime privilege. This is not a good idea! The board not only misses out on the opportunity to inject fresh blood into the institution, but also gives itself no recourse if it wants to fill that slot with someone else down the road. In addition, when a former chief executive is given board membership, it can pose conflicts for the succeeding chief executive, particularly if the former executive remains committed to doing things the old way and voices opposition to proposed changes.

The case study on page 73 can be used to spark board or committee discussion around the removal of ineffective board members. It is useful in stressing the importance of keeping board members interested and engaged. One of the goals of the exercise is for participants to understand the value of devoting time and resources to keeping board members focused on their responsibilities and on the organization's mission.

REMOVING A DIFFICULT BOARD MEMBER

Perhaps the most common reason for wanting to remove a board member is non-attendance or inactivity. But occasionally, a board member needs to be removed because he or she is preventing the board from doing its work. In some cases, a conflict of interest or unethical behavior may be grounds to remove an individual from the board. In other cases, a board member's behavior may become so obstructive that the board is prevented from functioning effectively. More frequently, the behavior of a problem board member discourages others from participating, and the board may find that other members attend less frequently or find reasons to resign.

Strongly felt disagreements, passionate arguments, and genuine debate are often elements of the most effective boards. Arguing for an unpopular viewpoint is not grounds for board dismissal. But if a board member consistently disrupts meetings, is unwilling to let the majority prevail, or prevents the organization from working well, it may be appropriate to consider removing the individual from the board.

Other reasons why a board may wish to remove a board member have to do with safe-guarding the organization's reputation and welfare. If a board member is indicted or convicted of illegal acts or takes public stands that are contrary to the organization's interest, the board might decide that it would be prudent to remove the person from the board.

Although board member removal is rare, organizations should provide for it in their bylaws. The following strategies can be used to remove troublesome board members:

- *Term Limits:* Term limits can provide a nonconfrontational way to ease ineffective board members off the board, while allowing terrific board members to be invited back after one or more years. Proponents feel that having a constant infusion of fresh thinking acts as a preventive measure for problem board members. Opponents of term limits believe that, with proper board leadership, errant board members can be guided toward either improving their behavior or quietly resigning from the board.

- *Personal Intervention:* If a board member has failed to fulfill his or her responsibilities, the board chair may take an opportunity to meet informally with the board member in question. In person or on the telephone, the board chair can discuss the matter with the person, and suggest that resignation may be appropriate. (Sometimes problem board members are relieved to have this as an option.)

- *Impeachment:* Organization bylaws should describe a process by which a board member can be removed by vote, if necessary. For example, missing three successive meetings may be reason for automatic removal from the board. However, unless this rule is uniformly enforced, with a troublesome board member it might lead to public accusations of discrimination. In some organizations, a board member can be removed by a two-thirds vote of the board at a regularly scheduled meeting.

Source: Adapted with permission from *The Best of Board Café* Copyright 2003. CompassPoint Nonprofit Services, published by and available from Fieldstone Alliance, 800-274-6024, www.FieldstoneAlliance.org. Free subscriptions to the *Board Café* newsletter at www.boardcafe.org.

STEP 8: ACTION STEPS

- Bring new members onto the board to ensure fresh insights and ideas and to prevent board members from going stale.

- Assign board members to different committees over time and provide opportunities for leadership roles to help keep board members interested.

- Balance the need for new members with the need for institutional memory and retention of valuable resources.

- Develop term-limit policies and be very intentional about the process of possible renomination.

- Practice great care when removing individual board members or even of the whole board. Be thoughtful of the people involved and ensure that legal guidelines are followed.

Step 9: Celebrate

In conscious celebration we create moments that illuminate the deeper meaning of our lives and guide our footsteps into the future.

— Cathy DeForest
  in *Transforming Leadership: From Vision to Results* by John D. Adams

APPRECIATE EFFORTS AND CELEBRATE ACHIEVEMENTS

While celebration is not actually a *step* in the board building cycle, it certainly is part of the process. Maybe a better way to describe it is a way of infusing a certain spirit of affirmation and hope into the steps involved in building an effective board. It needs to be part of everything a board does throughout the cycle to strengthen its performance and to add meaning to the lives of its members. Even as the board struggles to reconcile the organization's available resources with its needs, the board can find ways to rejoice. The trick is to recognize the things worth celebrating. Every board member — as well as every staff member who connects with the board — has a role to play in identifying the things that make people smile and that add energy to common tasks.

When board members do a good job, they deserve recognition. When the organization completes a project, when an individual board member has good news to share, or when the board has reached a milestone, it is important to take time out, even momentarily, to celebrate.

At the completion of a strategic planning process, the hiring of a new chief executive, or the resolution of a thorny issue, the board should set aside time to reflect on the things that contributed to the achievement and then celebrate the accomplishment. Often the long hours and extra efforts go overlooked and those who dedicated their time go unrecognized. When the organization experiences achievements, such as the passage of important legislation or a new grant award, the board should remember to applaud and express its appreciation to the staff and board members who were involved in making it happen.

How to appreciate and celebrate an individual board member's achievement is a matter that should be considered carefully and should be tailored to the individual involved. The board chair and chief executive may pay tribute to an individual board member in a variety of ways for a job well done, ranging from an informal but public "thank you" at a board meeting to a certificate or award at a special event or a special mention in the newsletter. However it is handled, the leadership should look for opportunities to recognize all members of the board for their unique contributions, even if they don't play particularly visible roles. Always being on time, helping with a fundraising event, or bringing important community issues to the attention of the chief executive are examples of subtle contributions. Organizing a meeting of community leaders to address a controversial issue or coordinating a successful educational event are examples of more noticeable achievements. Both kinds of support deserve a thank-you.

Expressing appreciation for a job well done is most effective when it is specific and not used to the extent that the recognition loses its value. Take care not to go overboard in honoring volunteer board service in general and do not praise someone for an achievement that was really accomplished by someone else. If a board member is praised for putting on a successful fundraising event, but everyone knows that the work was done by the staff, it may leave a bad taste in people's mouths and lead to cynicism rather than genuine appreciation.

PICK THE STYLE OF RECOGNITION

Celebration can take many forms, from the simple to the elaborate. The way in which a board chooses to recognize its members and celebrate its successes may depend upon the culture of the board, the budget allocated for board activities, and the geographical proximity that board members have to the organization. The following are some of the ways in which boards can show appreciation:

- *Special Events:* Board recognition events, which include board members and their spouses or significant others, can be elaborate dinners, a simple reception at someone's home, or a board and staff barbeque at a local park on a Saturday afternoon.

- *Tokens of Appreciation:* In recognition of everyone's faithful service, board members may receive useful items such as travel coffee mugs, special shirts, or umbrellas imprinted with the organization's logo. These gifts can be handed out at a board retreat or at the annual meeting.

- *Edible Treats:* Surprising the board with special refreshments in connection with a board meeting can help celebrate particular board or organizational achievements.

- *Raise a Glass:* Appreciation of those leaving the board at the end of their term can be simply and elegantly expressed by popping a cork and raising a glass of bubbly either alcoholic or nonalcoholic. This can also be repeated as a celebratory welcome when new members come to their first meeting.

One of the ways to continually strengthen the connections between board members is to begin every board meeting with five minutes of personal "good news." Ask board members to briefly share something significant from their own life since the last meeting. As they mention the graduation of children, births of grandchildren, vacations completed, promotions at work, etc., board members begin to identify with the things they have in common and the personal stories become real conversation starters during breaks and after meetings. After a while they begin to realize that they have a stake in each other's good news and they begin to truly feel like a team.

People who carry special responsibilities, such as the board chair or members with particularly challenging board assignments, need encouragement to counterbalance the times when they question why they took on the responsibility in the first place. It helps when others give them feedback, not just "you are doing a good job," but something more specific. For example, "I admired the way you were able to move us through that difficult discussion," or "Thanks for keeping our feet to the fire on that issue. We certainly did not make it easy for you!"

Formal ceremonies and official recognition are sometimes called for, but it is often the unexpected remembrances — the sudden applause or the single rose placed by one's seat at the table — that leave lasting impressions and that make it possible to keep going when the board faces challenges. Keep the celebrations fun and light and don't make them feel artificial. Forced conviviality does not work, but creating a climate of appreciation and laughter helps to generate the energy the board needs to get the job done.

Boards that make time for members to get to know one another, share stories, and compare experiences from their lives are more likely to work through their disagreements and find creative solutions. Boards that celebrate their potential for learning and growing and for making a difference in the world will attract the resources needed to carry out their mission. Celebration is not, therefore, the last step in the board building cycle — it is a spirit that should be infused in every step of the cycle for a lasting and successful outcome.

STEP 9: ACTION STEPS

- Motivate board member involvement and build momentum toward achieving goals by initiating opportunities for celebration.

- Find ways to actively appreciate the achievements of the organization, the board, and its members.

- Create opportunities whenever possible for recognizing good news and relationships, from very low key and informal moments to special events that might include family members and/or staff.

- Include good news from the personal or professional lives of board members. This can help deepen relationships, which in turn helps to better deal with differences and find creative solutions.

- Keep things light. Find ways to inject humor into the work of the board.

Case Studies

CASE STUDY 1

THE BOARD BUILDING CYCLE — WHERE DO YOU START?

The Hometown Organization is a thirty-year-old community service organization with programs in the areas of employment, housing, and education. It is located in an area that is scheduled for redevelopment and knows that it will have to relocate some time in the next several years. The organization's finances are stretched thin because of the increasing need for services caused by a downturn in the local economy after two major businesses shut their doors and a cut back in government support.

The board currently has 30 members. It meets for one hour every month, at which time several committees report on their work over the past month or two and the chief executive briefs the board on recent developments. For some time the board has had a hard time getting a quorum (50 percent of members). Board membership consists of 15 business people: three representatives from local churches, one appointed by the mayor, one appointed by the president of the community college, and the rest from the community-at-large. Their ages range from 43 to 75 and are fairly evenly divided between men and women. All but three are white.

The chair of the governance committee, Carolyn Carlson, had recently read a copy of the BoardSource publication, *The Board Building Cycle*, and had provided a copy for each of the other four committee members. This is their first meeting since the last election five months ago.

After calling the meeting to order, the chair recalls that it was not easy to find candidates to fill the open slots at the last election and how relieved everyone was that most of those eligible for re-election chose to stay on, even though some of them rarely came to meetings. At that point Karen Sweeney interrupts to ask about what had happened to a couple of the newly elected ones who did not come to the last two meetings — one of whom did not even attend the orientation luncheon with the chief executive. Kent Wilson reports that he too had noticed that attendance had been spotty for a number of members and that he himself sometimes did not come to meetings because of other demands on his time and because he did not think that it would matter if he was there or not.

"Well, this brings me to what I want us to talk about at this meeting," Carolyn says. "You have hopefully had a chance to read the book I sent you. What are the insights from the book that you think we need to consider?"

Questions

1. If you were a member of the Hometown governance committee, what would you suggest?

2. What steps can the committee implement on its own?

3. What issues should be raised with others? Who should be involved?

CASE STUDY 2

DEALING WITH INEFFECTIVE BOARD MEMBERS

Barbara Bartholomew just conducted her first meeting as chair of the nine-member board of a retirement community. Now in her fourth year on the board, Barbara headed the search committee to find a new chief executive two years earlier. Since then, she and Tom Moore, the chief executive, have created a future vision for expanded services that would move the organization into the top ranks of elder care facilities in their city. But to reach that objective will require hard work — plus major new resources. At this meeting, the board authorized a new capital campaign, the largest ever.

"We can't succeed unless we have more horsepower. We have nine people on the board. Six are jewels, but three are not pulling their weight," said Barbara to Tom as they left the meeting room. "We can't afford such deadwood."

"What can we do?" asked Tom. "You know even better than I the situation with those three people."

"I certainly do," said Barbara. She paused, then spoke again. "Number one is the granddaughter of the founder of this institution. She hardly ever attends a meeting. When she does, her ideas are archaic."

"Number two is the guy who 10 years ago made the largest gift ever to this facility. But he hasn't given a nickel since. Furthermore, he never says a single word at board meetings, or between board meetings for that matter."

"Number three? He's got an opinion about everything. He never shuts up at meetings, but he never follows through on any ideas. However, he's a partner in my husband's law firm."

Questions

1. What can Barbara do in the short term to begin to resolve the immediate problems with these three board members?

2. What actions could be taken by the board to avoid a similar situation in the future?

3. Other comments?

CASE STUDY 3

MAKING ROOM FOR A MORE DIVERSE BOARD

Clean-It-Up, a young, regional environmental protection organization, has a small, but strong and vibrant board. Last year the board adopted a strategic plan that identified the need for expanding beyond recycling and education to legislative advocacy and lobbying. While the board was very enthusiastic about adding this approach to its program, it also agreed that it lacked the expertise necessary to provide the guidance that would be necessary for success.

Board elections are coming up and the chair is meeting with the governance committee to consider nominations. The committee has identified the need for adding someone with grassroots lobbying experience and knowledge of the region's political landscape. Two committee members have just reported how excited they are to have identified two potential candidates with exactly the kinds of backgrounds and values the board is looking for. "The trouble is," says the chair, "that we don't have room for either of them unless we don't re-elect at least one of our current members who are up for re-election." "But we need these new folks if we are going to move forward with our new plan," adds someone, "we can't afford *not* to elect at least one of them!"

As the committee realizes that it has some hard choices to make, it considers each of the incumbents. One is badly needed because of her financial expertise and another for his connections to the wider environmental movement. The third is Frank Champo, one of the founding board members. He has a fine board record and is well liked by everyone on the board — he even makes a significant financial contribution every year. However, of the three he is the one who could be replaced without leaving a gaping hole, except for his institutional memory. "But I know that Frank wants to stay and is assuming that he will be re-elected," says the chair, "and I don't know that the rest of the board would have the heart to turn him down."

Questions

1. What are the options for dealing with the question of Frank Champo's re-election?

2. Does the board have options other than to choosing between Frank and one of the prospective new members in order to move forward on the new strategic initiative?

3. What might be the result of not making changes on the board this year?

Appendix

ABOUT THE CD-ROM

The CD-ROM includes documents featured in this book and a Microsoft®
PowerPoint® presentation called *Presenting: Board Orientation.*

The documents are provided in Microsoft® Word® and in plain text formats, and they
may be downloaded to be easily customized or used as is.

- Board Meeting Evaluation Form

- Sample Board Member Letter of Agreement

- Board Profile Worksheet

- Individual Board Member Self-Evaluation Form

- Mini Board Self-Assessment Survey

- Prospective Board Member Information Sheet

- Board Candidate Rating Form

- Board Member Orientation Checklist

Presenting: Board Orientation is a PowerPoint® presentation that can be customized to
fit your organization.

The slides in the presentation are divided into four sections:

- Section 1: Overview of the Nonprofit Sector

- Section 2: About the Organization

- Section 3: About the Board

- Section 4: Board Roles and Responsibilities

The slides are in PowerPoint® graphics presentation format that can be used as an
on-screen presentation, printed as overhead transparency slides, or handed out to the
board.

The files that accompany the presentation are:

- Customizing instructions for the PowerPoint® presentation

- Overview of *Presenting: Board Orientation*

- A text file that includes all of the information in the PowerPoint® presentation.

The text for the presentation is available in three formats:

Microsoft® PowerPoint®; Microsoft® Word® (included with the Overview); and plain
text. Use some or all of the sections depending on how they apply to your nonprofit
and the time you have allotted for the orientation.

SUGGESTED RESOURCES

Assessment for Nonprofit Governing Boards. Washington, DC: BoardSource, 2003. The *Assessment for Nonprofit Governing Boards* helps nonprofit governing boards determine how well they are carrying out their responsibilities and identifies areas that need improvement. Board members complete the confidential online questionnaires to evaluate the board's performance as well as their own contributions. Your board members' responses will help identify the strengths and weaknesses of your current board with questions focused on 10 key areas of board responsibility.

BoardSource. *The Source: Twelve Principles of Governance That Power Exceptional Boards.* Washington, DC: BoardSource, 2005. Exceptional boards add significant value to their organizations, making discernible differences in their advance on mission. *The Source* defines governance not as dry, obligatory compliance, but as a creative and collaborative process that supports chief executives, engages board members, and furthers the causes they all serve. It enables nonprofit boards to operate at the highest and best use of their collective capacity. Aspirational in nature, these principles offer chief executives a description of an empowered board that is a strategic asset to be leveraged, and provide board members with a vision of what is possible and a way to add lasting value to the organizations they lead.

Hopkins, Bruce R. *Legal Responsibilities of Nonprofit Boards.* Washington, DC: BoardSource, 2003. All board members should understand their legal responsibilities, including when and how they can be held personally liable and what type of oversight they should provide. Discover the essential information that board members should know to protect themselves and their organization. Written in nontechnical language, this booklet provides legal concepts and definitions, as well as a detailed discussion on ethics.

Ingram, Richard T. *Ten Basic Responsibilities of Nonprofit Boards.* Washington, DC: BoardSource, 2003. More than 150,000 board members have already discovered this #1 BoardSource bestseller. This revised edition explores the 10 core areas of board responsibility. Share with board members the basic responsibilities, including determining mission and purpose, ensuring effective planning, and participating in fundraising. You'll find that this is an ideal reference for drafting job descriptions, assessing board performance, and orienting board members on their responsibilities.

Lakey, Berit M., Sandra R. Hughes, and Outi Flynn. *Governance Committee.* Washington, DC: BoardSource, 2004. Governance committees are essential in every board because of their ability to ensure full board effectiveness. This book illustrates how a governance committee not only recruits new members, but also transforms those recruits into productive and capable board embers. The authors outline duties of the governance committee and provide helpful hints and guidelines on who should serve on this committee, how to determine what kinds of members your board needs, where to find these individuals, and how to orient and continuously educate your board.

Lawrence, Barbara and Outi Flynn. *The Nonprofit Policy Sampler.* Washington, DC: BoardSource, 2006. *The Nonprofit Policy Sampler* is designed to help board and staff leaders advance their organizations, make better collective decisions, and guide individual actions and behaviors. This tool provides key elements and practical tips for 48 topic areas, along with more than 240 sample policies, job descriptions, committee charters, codes of ethics, board member agreements, mission and vision statements, and more. Each topic includes anywhere from two to 13 sample documents so that nonprofit leaders can select an appropriate sample from which to start drafting or revising their own policy. All samples are professionally and legally reviewed. Samples are included on CD-ROM.

Meeting the Challenge: An Orientation to Nonprofit Board Service. Video. Washington, DC: BoardSource, 1998. Hosted by Ray Suarez, the former voice of National Public Radio's Talk of the Nation and former board member for the Chicago Council of Boy Scouts, this video highlights the four basic principles of board responsibility — determining mission and program, ensuring effective oversight, providing resources, and participating in community outreach. The video features interviews with board members, chief executives, and experts in the field of board governance as they share their experiences and insights into nonprofit board service.

About the Author

During more than 30 years in consulting, training, communications, and nonprofit management, **Berit M. Lakey, Ph.D.**, has acquired unique insights into the complex nature of nonprofit organizations. Her diverse roles include that of teacher, trainer, staff administrator, author, executive director, and board member. As a consultant, she has focused primarily on issues of governance working with health and human services organizations, foundations, credit unions, religious and arts organizations, and associations. She has also served as an adjunct assistant professor in the graduate school at University of Maryland University College.

Lakey joined BoardSource in 1991 and served as a senior staff consultant for six years. She now works as an independent consultant and continues to take on assignments for BoardSource along with other clients in the United States and abroad. She provides individualized board consulting and training, conducts workshops for board members and board consultants, and facilitates board self-assessments.

She holds a master's degree in organizational development and a doctorate in human and organizational systems from the Fielding Graduate University in Santa Barbara, California. She resides in Silver Spring, Maryland.